RICHMOND

Picture Dictionary

ENGLISH - SPANISH

SPANISH - ENGLISH

Richmond PUBLISHING

SANTILLANA

Printed in Colombia. Impreso en Colombia por D'vinni S.A.

ISBN 10: 1-58105-260-x
ISBN 13: 978-1-58105-260-2

10 09 08   14 15 16 17 18 19 20

CONTENTS/CONTENIDO

INTRODUCTION/INTRODUCCIÓN

The **Richmond Picture Dictionary** has been designed so that young students may use it at home or in school during their first years of studying English or Spanish. It was planned to help students establish an immediate association between vocabulary and a visual image. In this way dependency on translation can be reduced. The dictionary offers students the opportunity of increasing and enriching their vocabulary through the association of the terms with their illustrations. It also builds confidence by providing an English-Spanish and a Spanish-English glossary at the end to help students learn to use a regular dictionary.

El **Richmond Picture Dictionary** ha sido diseñado para que jóvenes estudiantes lo usen de manera independiente en casa o en el colegio durante sus primeros años de aprendizaje del inglés o del español. El diccionario está concebido para ayudar a los estudiantes a establecer una asociación inmediata entre el vocabulario y una imagen visual; de esta manera se reduce la dependencia de la traducción. El diccionario ofrece a los estudiantes la oportunidad de aumentar y enriquecer su vocabulario a través de la asociación de los términos con las ilustraciones. Asimismo les transmite seguridad al proporcionar un glosario inglés-español y otro español-inglés que les ayuda a familiarizarse con los diccionarios convencionales.

VISUAL VOCABULARY/VOCABULARIO VISUAL

The Visual Vocabulary section presents words from 17 topics that are divided into 72 different subcategories. The full color drawings were computer generated to offer a three-dimentional look and show each object in great detail. The drawings are classified in two groups: those that represent objects, living things or discriptions, and those that represent actions. Nouns, verbs, and adjectives are each illustrated separately.
At home or in school, students can copy elements from certain drawing to create their own homework or vocabulary notes. In the classroom, games can be organized in which the teacher, and then the students, first describe the object and its place in the drawing, and then ask the other students to name it.

La sección del Vocabulario visual presenta las palabras en 17 temas que se dividen en 72 subcategorías diferentes. Los dibujos, a todo color, han sido generados con computadoras para darle una apariencia tridimensional y mostrar cada objeto con gran detalle. Los dibujos se clasifican claramente con las palabras para objetos, seres vivos, descripciones y acciones. Los nombres, verbos y adjetivos se ilustran cada uno por separado.
En casa o en la escuela, los estudiantes pueden copiar elementos de determinados dibujos para producir sus propias tarjetas o apuntes de vocabulario. En la clase, el/la profesor/a puede organizar juegos en los cuales el/la profesor/a y después los estudiantes, primero describen un objeto y su localización en el dibujo, y después piden a los demás estudiantes que lo nombren.

DAN AND PAM

Dan and Pam are two characters that appear on almost every page of the Visual Vocabulary section. Their purpose is to represent the relevant actions for the topic on each page and reinforce their meaning using gestures and expressions. The teacher can take advantage of the actions that Dan and Pam present to play imitations games or other activities or to develop narratives.

Dan y Pam son dos personajes que aparecen en casi todas las páginas de la sección del Vocabulario visual. Su propósito es el de representar las acciones relevantes para el tema de cada página y reforzar el significado por medio de gestos y expresiones.
El/la profesor/a puede sacar provecho de las acciones que presentan Dan y Pam para juegos de imitación u otras actividades, o para el desarrollo de narraciones.

GLOSSARY/GLOSARIO

In the glossary all the words that appear in the Visual Vocabulary are in alphabetical order. Each word is translated just as it is shown in the drawing. The English terms are standard American English. The Spanish terms are those that appear in the Visual Vocabulary section; however, regional Spanish variants are also given. In case of doubt, each illustrated word has a page number for your reference.

En la sección del glosario, todas las palabras que aparecen en el Vocabulario visual están dispuestas alfabéticamente. Los términos en inglés representan el inglés americano. Los términos en español representan el español americano. A estos últimos se les agregan las variantes regionales más comunes. Cada palabra ilustrada lleva una referencia a la página de la ilustración.

VISUAL
VOCABULARY

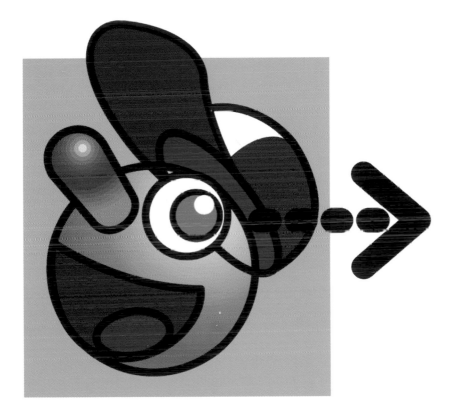

VOCABULARIO
VISUAL

Parts of the body/Partes del cuerpo

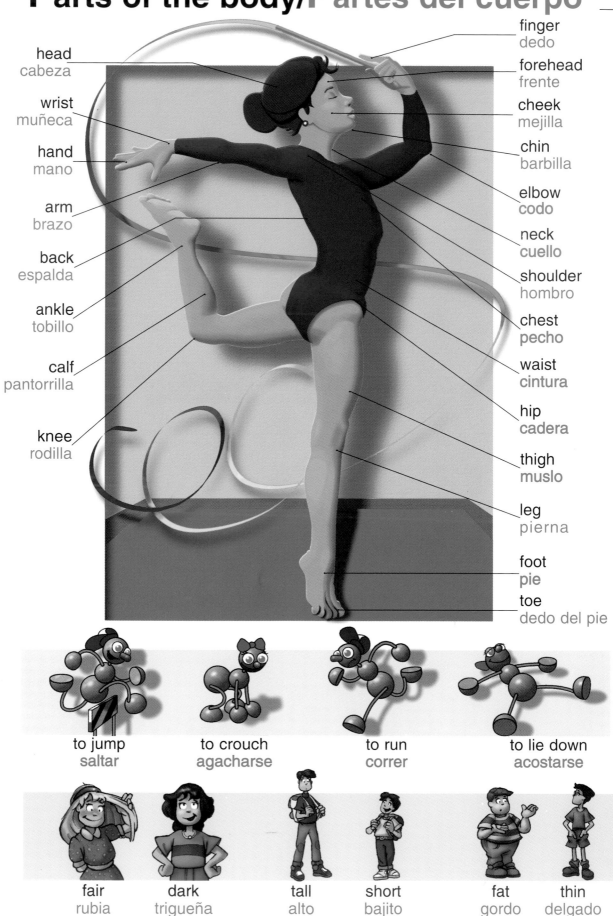

head
cabeza

wrist
muñeca

hand
mano

arm
brazo

back
espalda

ankle
tobillo

calf
pantorrilla

knee
rodilla

finger
dedo

forehead
frente

cheek
mejilla

chin
barbilla

elbow
codo

neck
cuello

shoulder
hombro

chest
pecho

waist
cintura

hip
cadera

thigh
muslo

leg
pierna

foot
pie

toe
dedo del pie

to jump
saltar

to crouch
agacharse

to run
correr

to lie down
acostarse

fair
rubia

dark
trigueña

tall
alto

short
bajito

fat
gordo

thin
delgado

Skeleton and muscles
Esqueleto y músculos

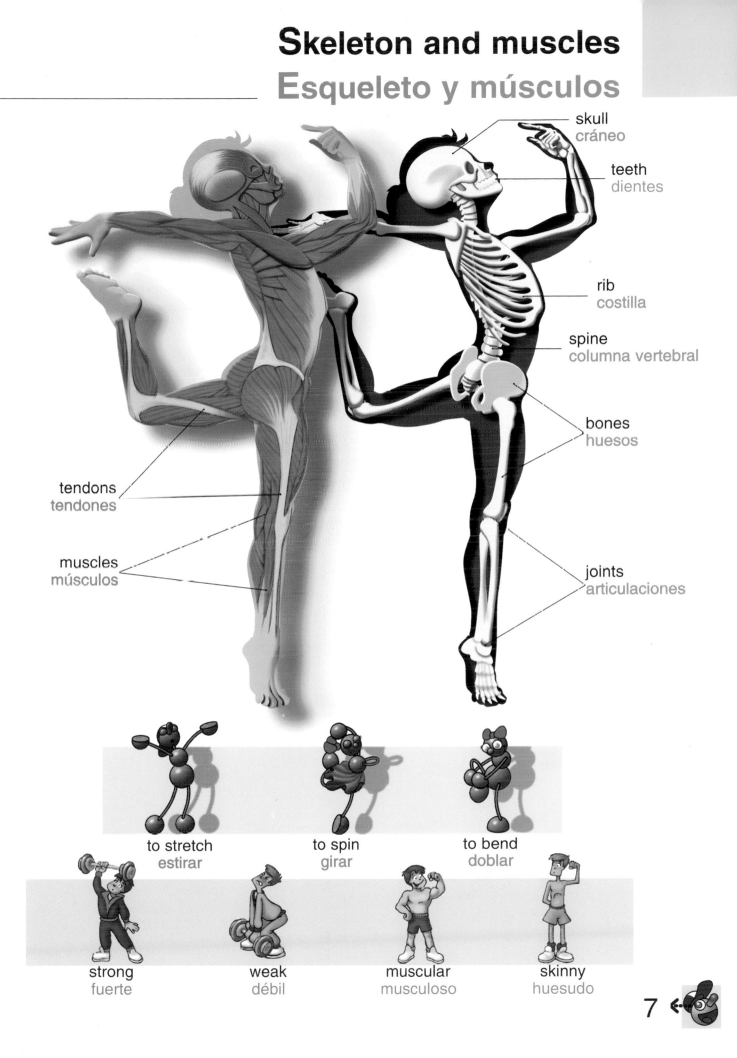

skull
cráneo

teeth
dientes

rib
costilla

spine
columna vertebral

bones
huesos

tendons
tendones

muscles
músculos

joints
articulaciones

to stretch
estirar

to spin
girar

to bend
doblar

strong
fuerte

weak
débil

muscular
musculoso

skinny
huesudo

Senses/Sentidos

sense of hearing
sentido del oído

ear
oreja

sense of smell
sentido del olfato

nose
nariz

nostril
fosa nasal

sense of touch
sentido del tacto

skin
piel

to touch
tocar

to taste
probar

to see
ver

to hear
oír

to smell
oler

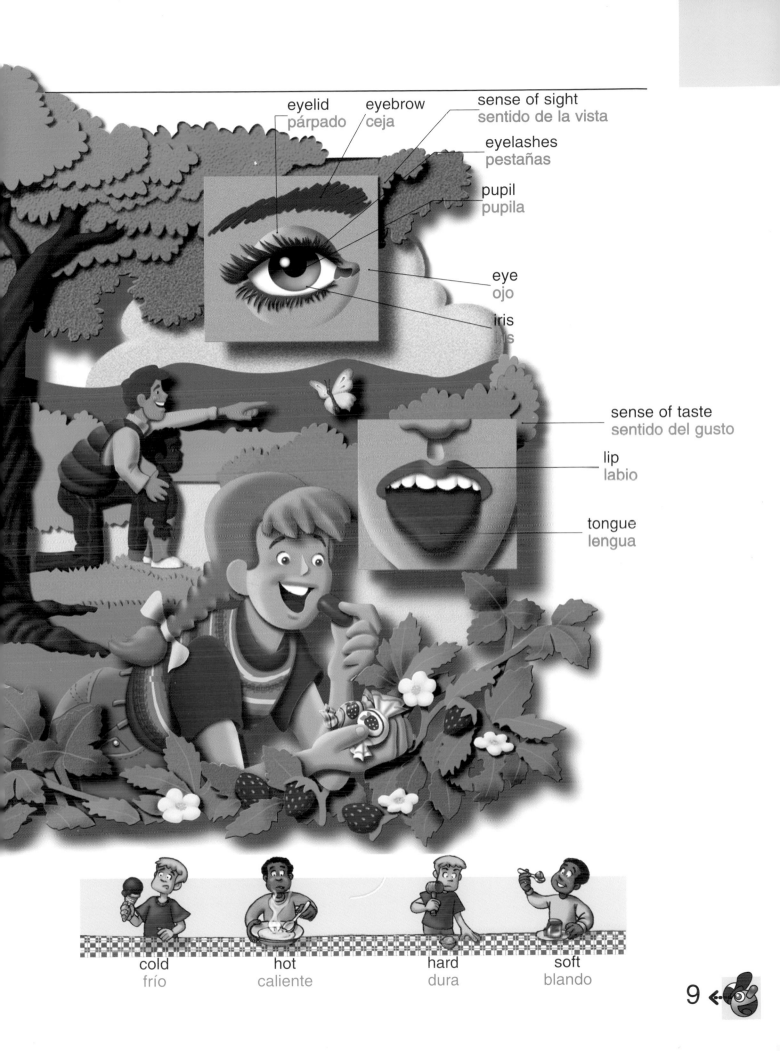

eyelid
párpado

eyebrow
ceja

sense of sight
sentido de la vista

eyelashes
pestañas

pupil
pupila

eye
ojo

iris
iris

sense of taste
sentido del gusto

lip
labio

tongue
lengua

cold
frío

hot
caliente

hard
dura

soft
blando

THE FAMILY/LA FAMILIA
Relatives/Parientes

father
padre

mother
madre

grandfather
abuelo

grandmother
abuela

sister
hermana

uncle
tío

aunt
tía

son
hijo

cousin
primo

brother
hermano

to love
querer

to shout
gritar

to laugh
reír

to cry
llorar

young
joven

old
vieja

happy
contenta

sad
triste

quiet
tranquilo

noisy
ruidoso

Parties/Fiestas familiares

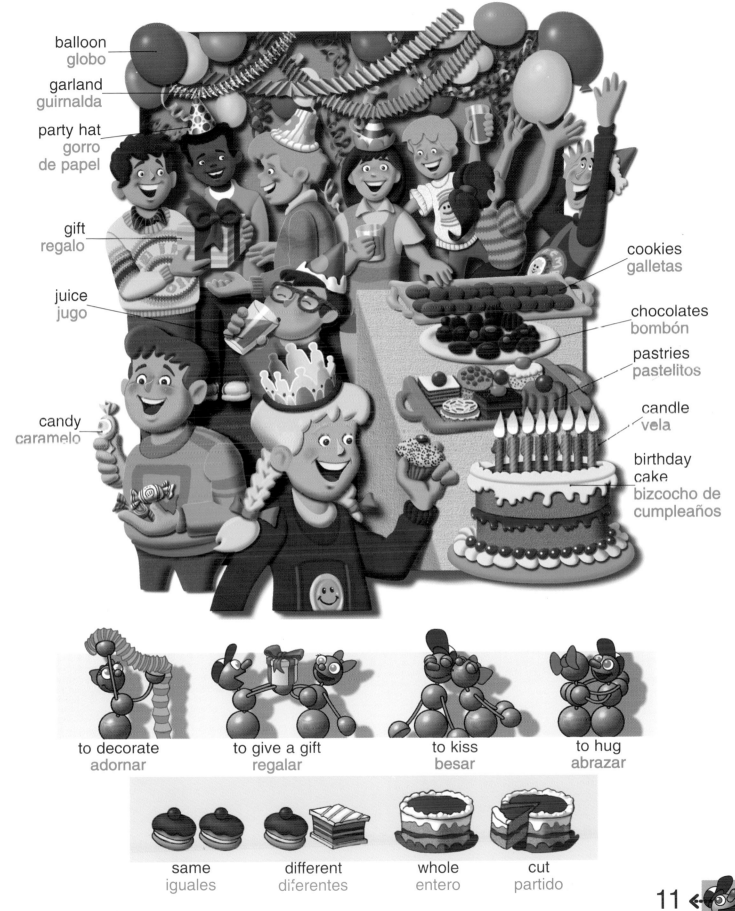

balloon
globo

garland
guirnalda

party hat
gorro
de papel

gift
regalo

juice
jugo

candy
caramelo

cookies
galletas

chocolates
bombón

pastries
pastelitos

candle
vela

birthday
cake
bizcocho de
cumpleaños

to decorate
adornar

to give a gift
regalar

to kiss
besar

to hug
abrazar

same
iguales

different
diferentes

whole
entero

cut
partido

CLOTHES/LA ROPA
Daytime/Para la calle

beret
boina

cap
gorra

sweater
suéter

blouse
blusa

belt
cinturón

skirt
falda

tights
leotardos

shoe
zapato

jacket
chaqueta

sweater
suéter

pants
pantalón

sock
media

athletic
shoe
zapato
deportivo

to get dressed
vestirse

to get undressed
desvestirse

to button up
abrocharse

to unbutton
desabrocharse

short
corta

long
larga

wrinkled
arrugada

ironed
planchada

12

Bedtime/Para dormir

T-shirt
camiseta

robe
bata

nightgown
camisón

pajamas
pijama

panties
pantaloncito

slipper
pantufla

underpants
calzoncillo

to put on
ponerse

to take off
quitarse

dirty
sucia

clean
limpia

tight
apretado

baggy
flojo

Outside/La casa por fuera

satellite dish
antena
de satélite

wall
pared

door
puerta

window
ventana

chimney
chimenea

roof
techo

garage
garaje

trash bin
basurero

fence
cerca

doorbell
timbre

dog house
perrera

steps
escalera

to lean out
asomarse

to go up
subir

to go down
bajar

to wallpaper
empapelar

new
nueva

old
vieja

close together
juntas

far apart
separadas

Living room/Sala

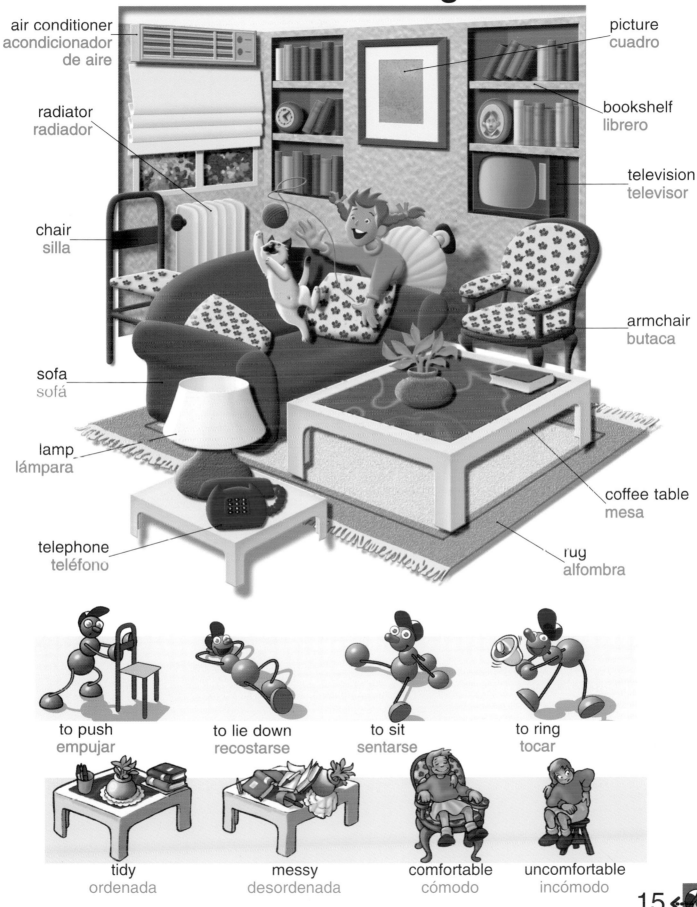

air conditioner
acondicionador
de aire

radiator
radiador

chair
silla

sofa
sofá

lamp
lámpara

telephone
teléfono

picture
cuadro

bookshelf
librero

television
televisor

armchair
butaca

coffee table
mesa

rug
alfombra

to push
empujar

to lie down
recostarse

to sit
sentarse

to ring
tocar

tidy
ordenada

messy
desordenada

comfortable
cómodo

uncomfortable
incómodo

15

Bedroom/**D**ormitorio

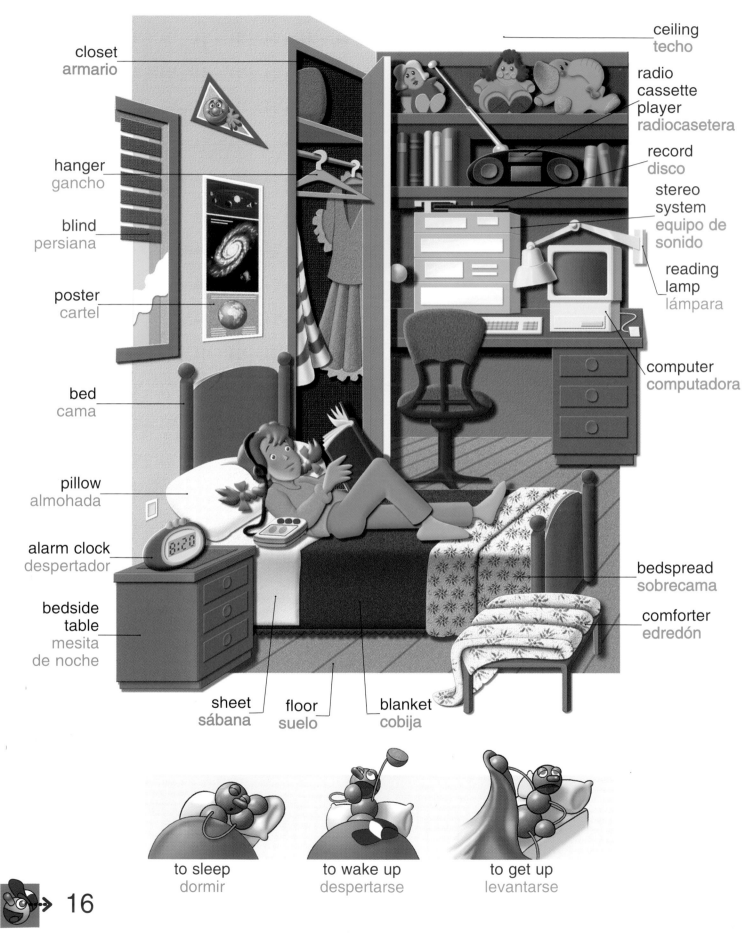

closet
armario

hanger
gancho

blind
persiana

poster
cartel

bed
cama

pillow
almohada

alarm clock
despertador

bedside
table
mesita
de noche

ceiling
techo

radio
cassette
player
radiocasetera

record
disco

stereo
system
equipo de
sonido

reading
lamp
lámpara

computer
computadora

bedspread
sobrecama

comforter
edredón

sheet
sábana

floor
suelo

blanket
cobija

to sleep
dormir

to wake up
despertarse

to get up
levantarse

Bathroom/Cuarto de baño

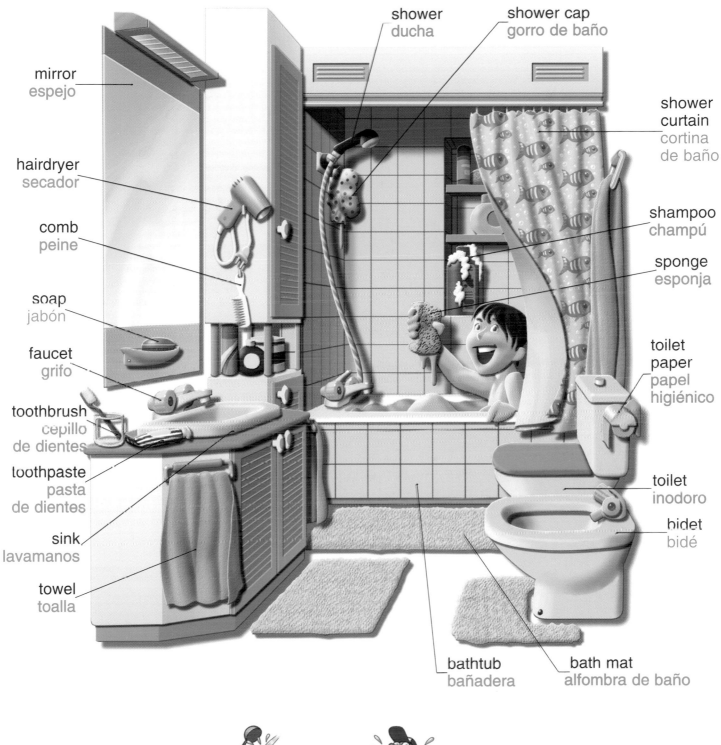

shower
ducha

shower cap
gorro de baño

mirror
espejo

shower curtain
cortina de baño

hairdryer
secador

shampoo
champú

comb
peine

sponge
esponja

soap
jabón

faucet
grifo

toilet paper
papel higiénico

toothbrush
cepillo de dientes

toothpaste
pasta de dientes

toilet
inodoro

sink
lavamanos

bidet
bidé

towel
toalla

bathtub
bañadera

bath mat
alfombra de baño

to brush your teeth
cepillarse los dientes

to take a shower
ducharse

dry yourself
secarse

to comb your hair
peinarse

Kitchen/Cocina

vase
florero

juicer
exprimidora

coffeemaker
cafetera

blender
licuadora

washing machine
lavadora

grater
rallador

table
mesa

corkcrew
sacacorchos

can opener
abrelatas

sink
fregadero

refrigerator
refrigerador

fork
tenedor

glass
vaso

soup bowl
plato hondo

plate
plato llano

bowl
bol

knife
cuchillo

spoon
cuchara

to stir
revolver

to grate
rallar

to cut
cortar

to chop
picar

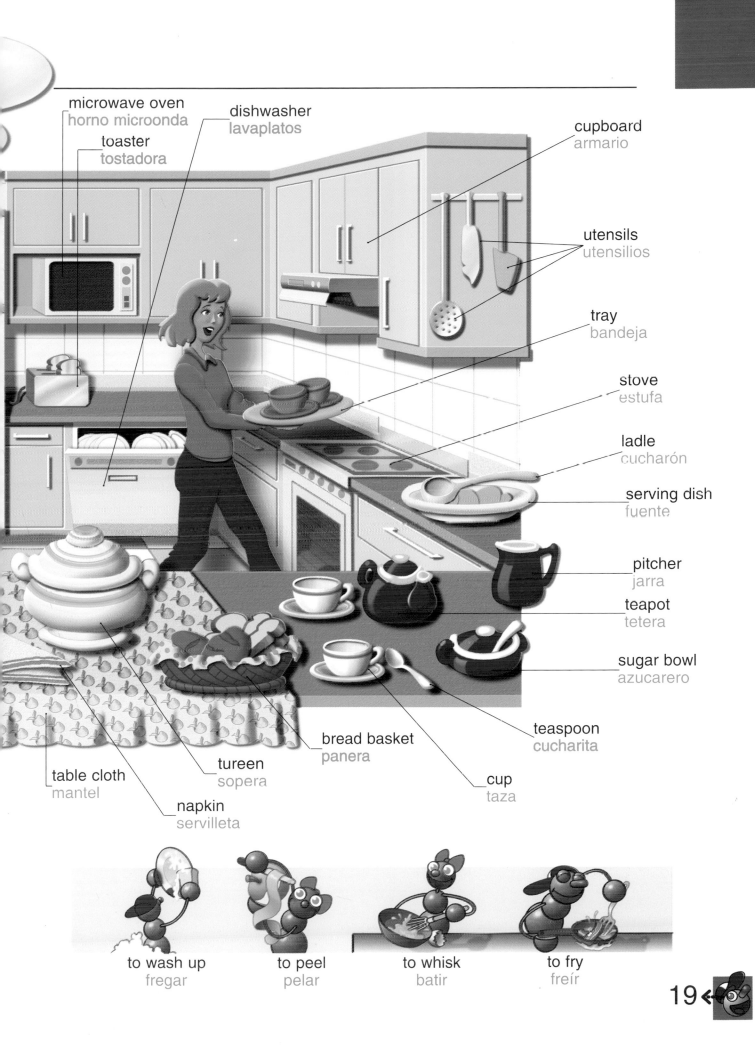

microwave oven
horno microonda

toaster
tostadora

dishwasher
lavaplatos

cupboard
armario

utensils
utensilios

tray
bandeja

stove
estufa

ladle
cucharón

serving dish
fuente

pitcher
jarra

teapot
tetera

sugar bowl
azucarero

teaspoon
cucharita

cup
taza

bread basket
panera

tureen
sopera

table cloth
mantel

napkin
servilleta

to wash up
fregar

to peel
pelar

to whisk
batir

to fry
freír

Where are they?/¿Dónde están?

in front
enfrente

above
arriba

below
abajo

near
cerca

on
encima

under
debajo

far
lejos

to overtake
adelantarse

to face
enfrentarse

to go away
alejarse

to approach
acercarse

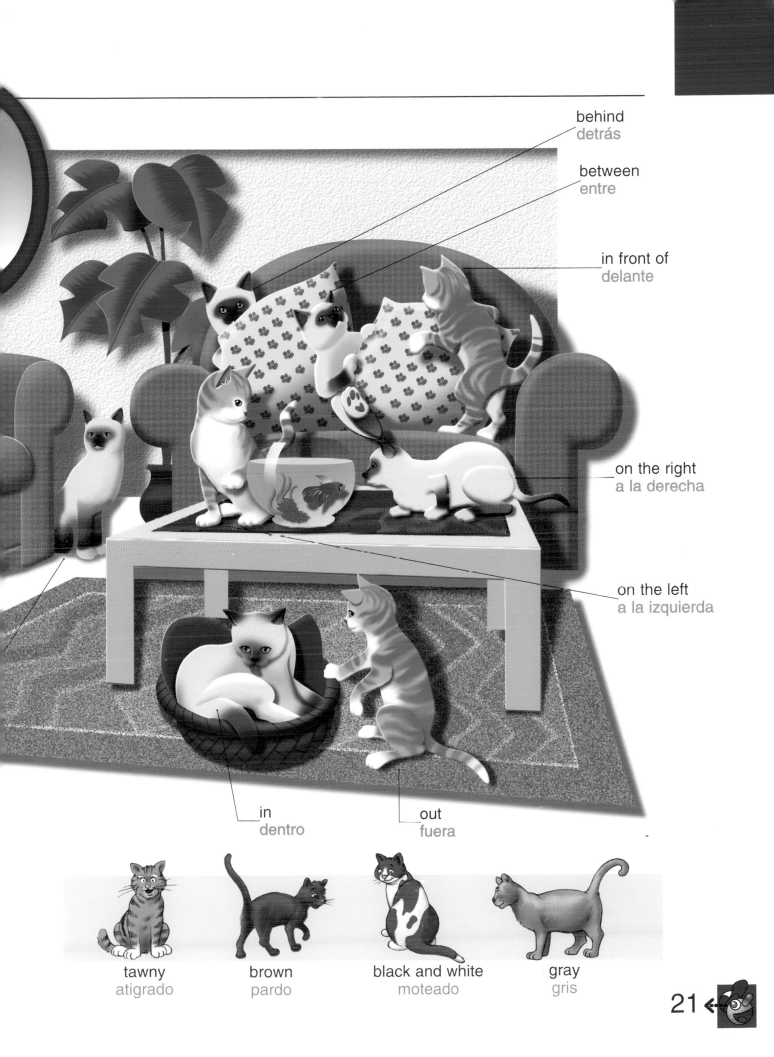

behind
detrás

between
entre

in front of
delante

on the right
a la derecha

on the left
a la izquierda

in
dentro

out
fuera

tawny
atigrado

brown
pardo

black and white
moteado

gray
gris

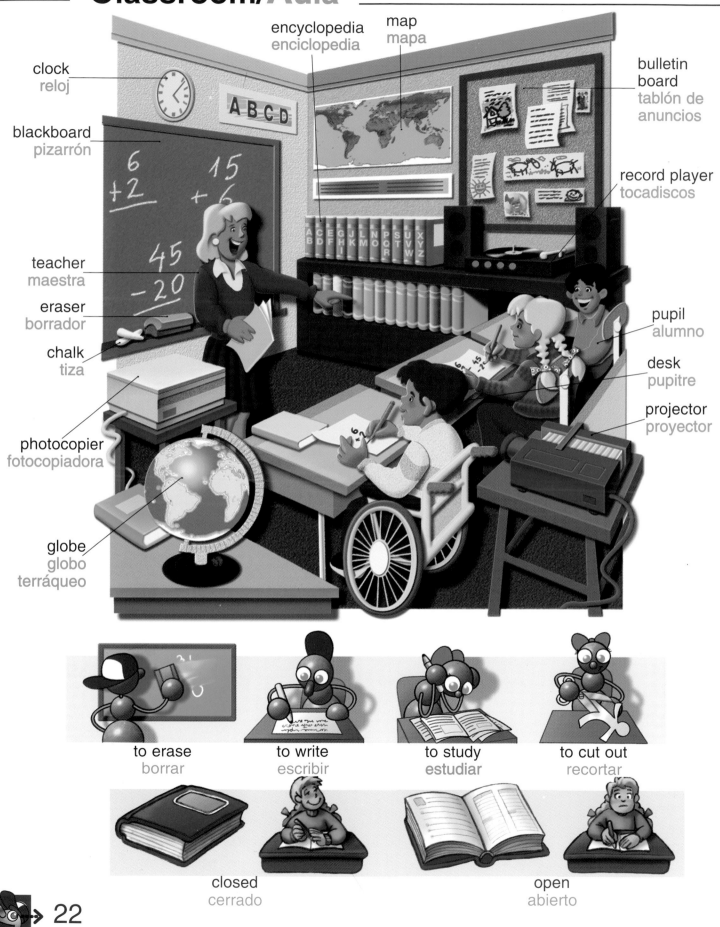

encyclopedia
enciclopedia

map
mapa

clock
reloj

bulletin board
tablón de anuncios

blackboard
pizarrón

record player
tocadiscos

teacher
maestra

eraser
borrador

pupil
alumno

chalk
tiza

desk
pupitre

projector
proyector

photocopier
fotocopiadora

globe
globo terráqueo

to erase
borrar

to write
escribir

to study
estudiar

to cut out
recortar

closed
cerrado

open
abierto

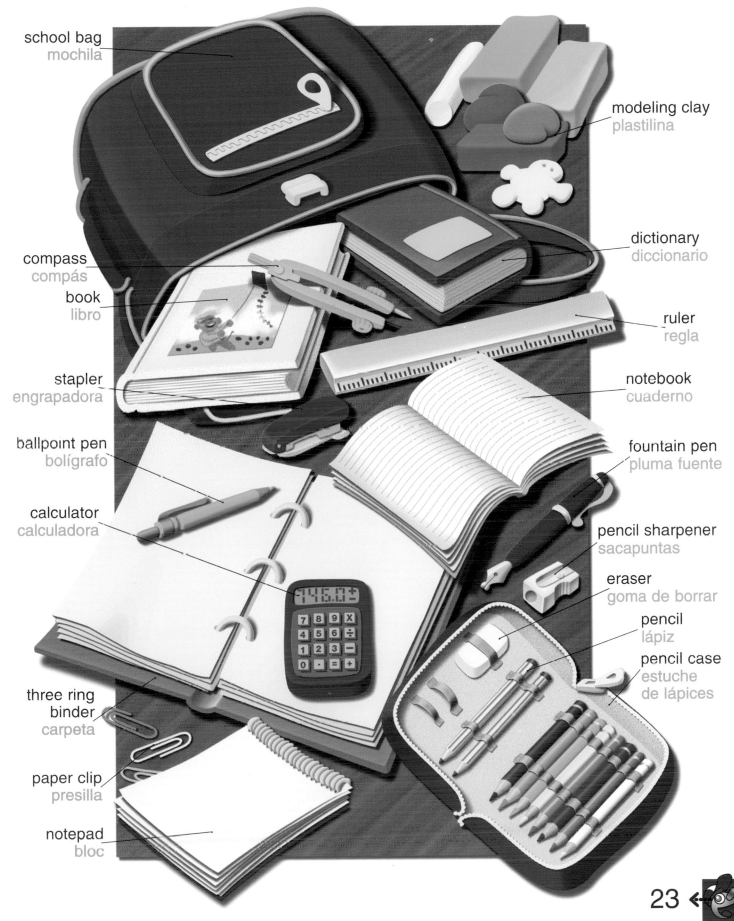

school bag
mochila

modeling clay
plastilina

dictionary
diccionario

compass
compás

book
libro

ruler
regla

stapler
engrapadora

notebook
cuaderno

ballpoint pen
bolígrafo

fountain pen
pluma fuente

calculator
calculadora

pencil sharpener
sacapuntas

eraser
goma de borrar

pencil
lápiz

pencil case
estuche
de lápices

three ring
binder
carpeta

paper clip
presilla

notepad
bloc

Colors/Colores

rainbow
arco iris

gray
gris

pink
rosado

brown
café

green
verde

orange
anaranjado

to draw
dibujar

to paint
pintar

to scribble
garabatear

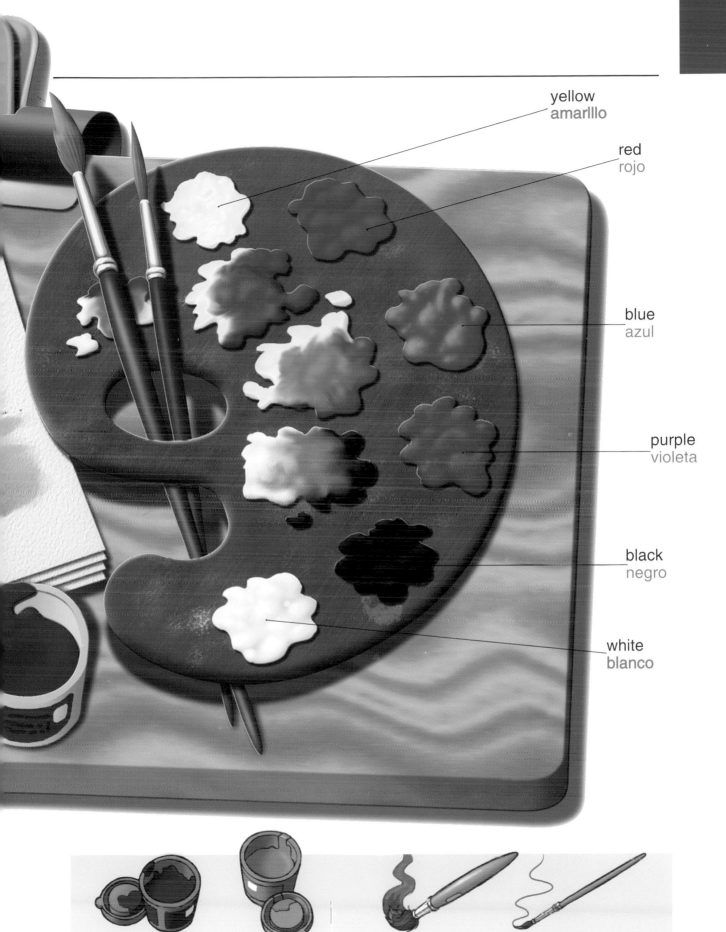

yellow
amarlllo

red
rojo

blue
azul

purple
violeta

black
negro

white
blanco

dark
oscuro

light
claro

thick
grueso

fine
fino

Numbers and shapes/Números y formas

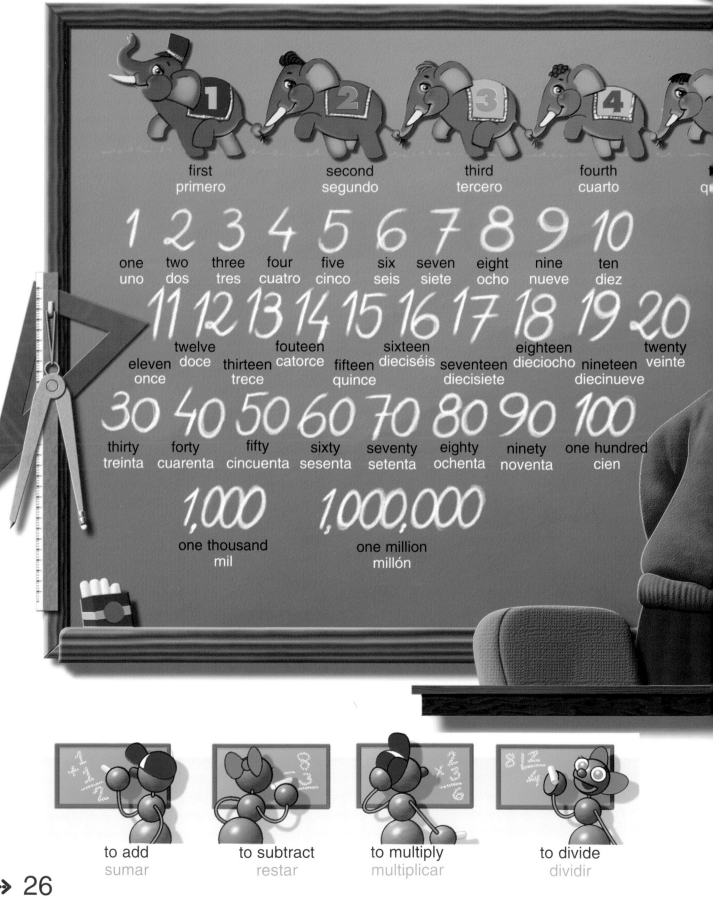

first	second	third	fourth
primero	segundo	tercero	cuarto

1	2	3	4	5	6	7	8	9	10
one	two	three	four	five	six	seven	eight	nine	ten
uno	dos	tres	cuatro	cinco	seis	siete	ocho	nueve	diez

11	12	13	14	15	16	17	18	19	20
eleven	twelve	thirteen	fouteen	fifteen	sixteen	seventeen	eighteen	nineteen	twenty
once	doce	trece	catorce	quince	dieciséis	diecisiete	dieciocho	diecinueve	veinte

30	40	50	60	70	80	90	100
thirty	forty	fifty	sixty	seventy	eighty	ninety	one hundred
treinta	cuarenta	cincuenta	sesenta	setenta	ochenta	noventa	cien

1,000	1,000,000
one thousand	one million
mil	millón

to add	to subtract	to multiply	to divide
sumar	restar	multiplicar	dividir

sixth
sexto

seventh
séptimo

eighth
octavo

ninth
noveno

tenth
décimo

cube
cubo

square
cuadrado

rectangle
rectángulo

sphere
esfera

cone
cono

circle
círculo

triangle
triángulo

round
redondo

rectangular
rectangular

triangular
triangular

square
cuadrada

brachiosaurus
braquiosaurio

diplodocus
diplodoco

parasaurolophus
parasaurolophus

triceratops
triceratops

to hatch
nacer

to swim
nadar

to fly
volar

to die
morir

archaeopteryx
arqueópterix

tyrannosaurus
tiranosaurio

stegosaurus
estegosaurio

compsognathus
compsognathus

carnivorous
carnívoro

herbivorous
herbívoro

light
ligero

heavy
pesado

gigantic
gigantesco

Dog and Cat/Perro y gato

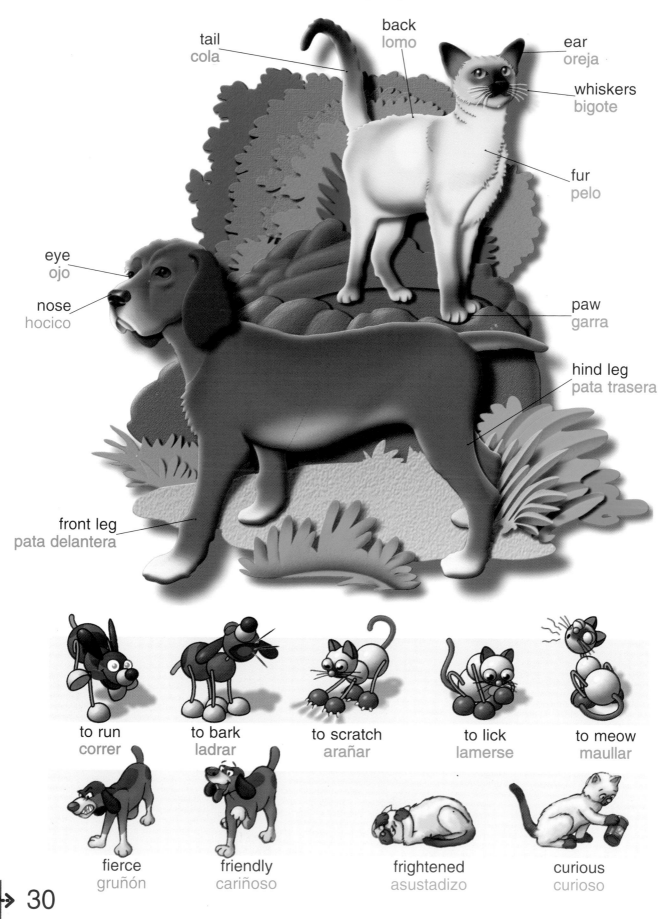

tail
cola

back
lomo

ear
oreja

whiskers
bigote

fur
pelo

eye
ojo

nose
hocico

paw
garra

hind leg
pata trasera

front leg
pata delantera

to run
correr

to bark
ladrar

to scratch
arañar

to lick
lamerse

to meow
maullar

fierce
gruñón

friendly
cariñoso

frightened
asustadizo

curious
curioso

Horse and Camel/Caballo y camello

hump
joroba

lip
labio

teeth
dientes

neck
cuello

mane
crin

back
lomo

foal
potro

hoof
casco

to trot
trotar

to neigh
relinchar

to gallop
galopar

tame
manso

wild
salvaje

Cow and sheep/Vaca y oveja

pen
corral

wool
lana

flock
rebaño

lamb
cordero

horn
cuerno

hide
piel

udder
ubre

hoof
pezuña

calf
ternero

to moo
mugir

to milk
ordeñar

to bleat
balar

to shear
esquilar

woolly
lanuda

playful
juguetón

obedient
obediente

Hen and Sparrow/Gallina y gorrión

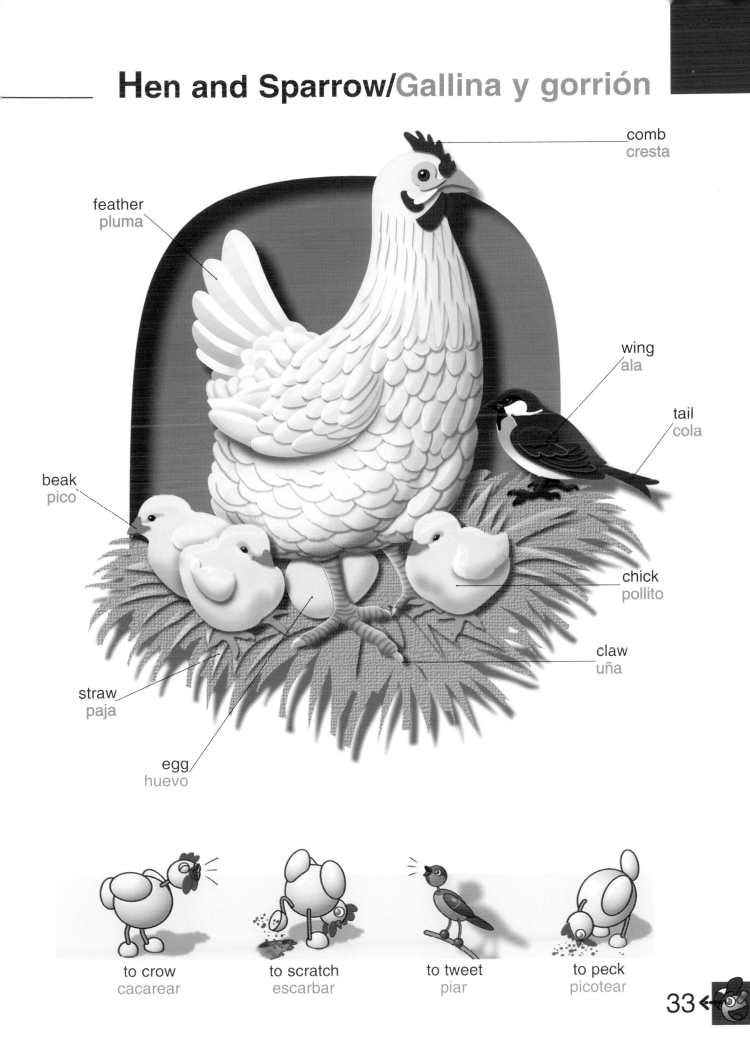

comb
cresta

feather
pluma

wing
ala

tail
cola

beak
pico

chick
pollito

claw
uña

straw
paja

egg
huevo

to crow
cacarear

to scratch
escarbar

to tweet
piar

to peck
picotear

Snake and tortoise/Serpiente y tortuga

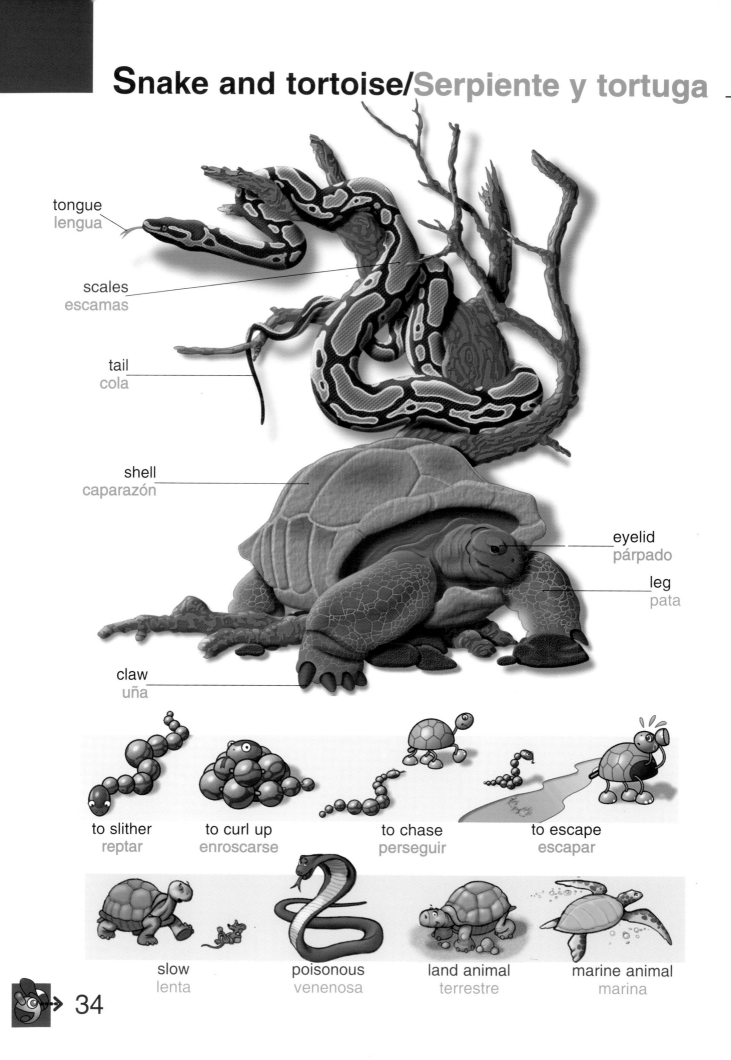

tongue
lengua

scales
escamas

tail
cola

shell
caparazón

eyelid
párpado

leg
pata

claw
uña

to slither
reptar

to curl up
enroscarse

to chase
perseguir

to escape
escapar

slow
lenta

poisonous
venenosa

land animal
terrestre

marine animal
marina

Shark and sardine/Tiburón y sardina

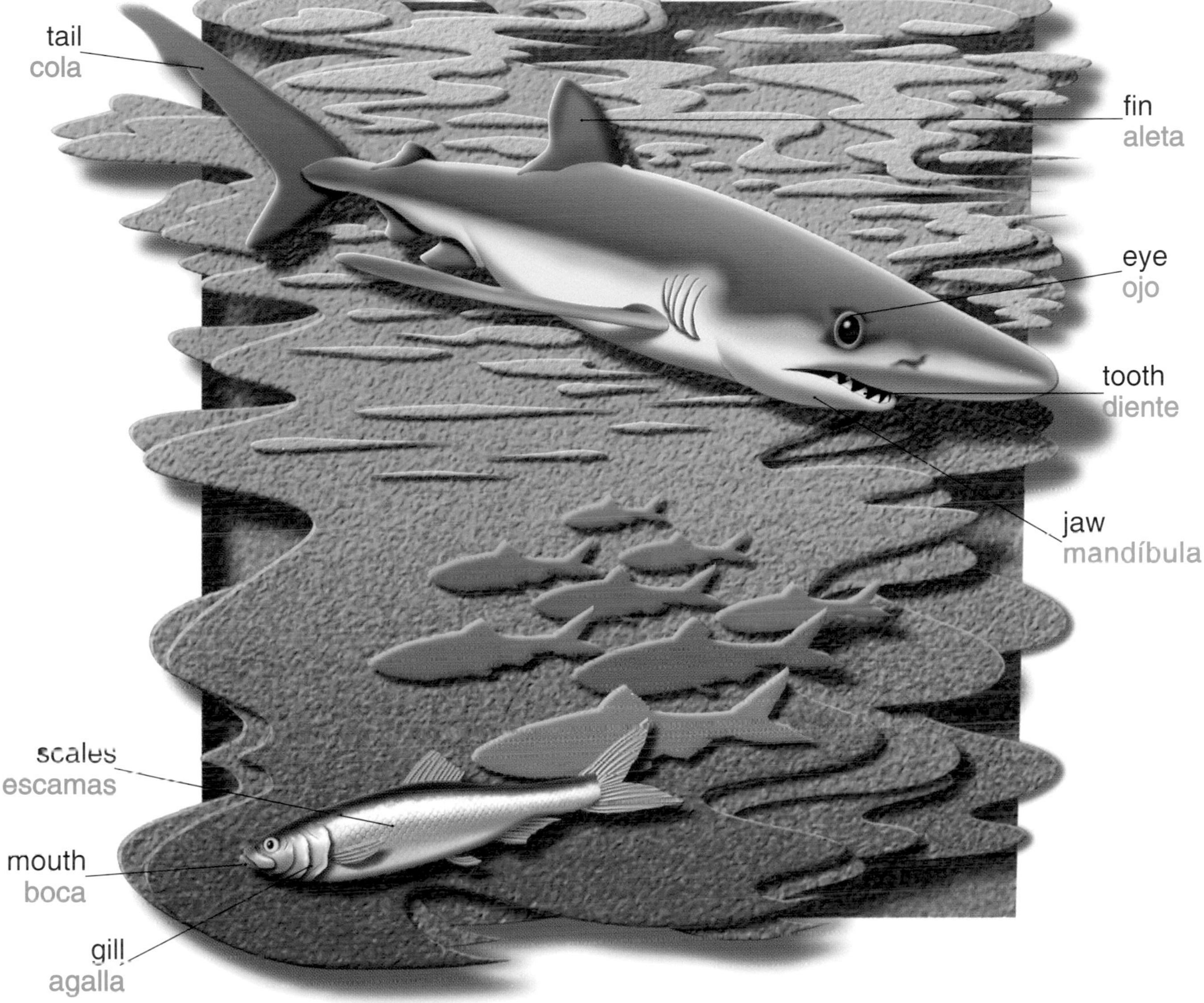

tail
cola

fin
aleta

eye
ojo

tooth
diente

jaw
mandíbula

scales
escamas

mouth
boca

gill
agalla

to look out
vigilar

to attack
atacar

to swallow
tragar

to fish
pescar

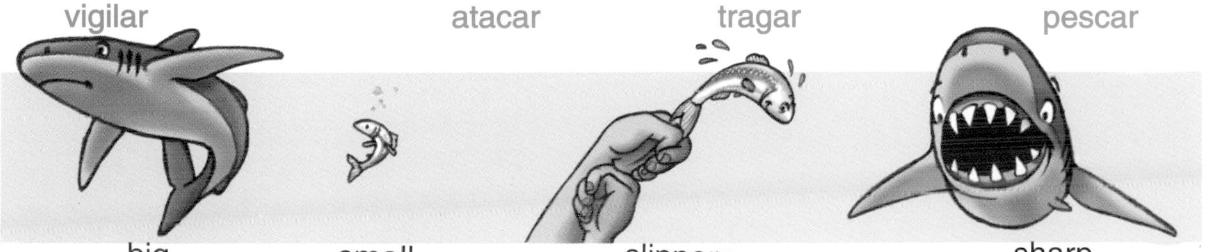

big
grande

small
pequeño

slippery
resbaladizo

sharp
afilados

Frog/Rana

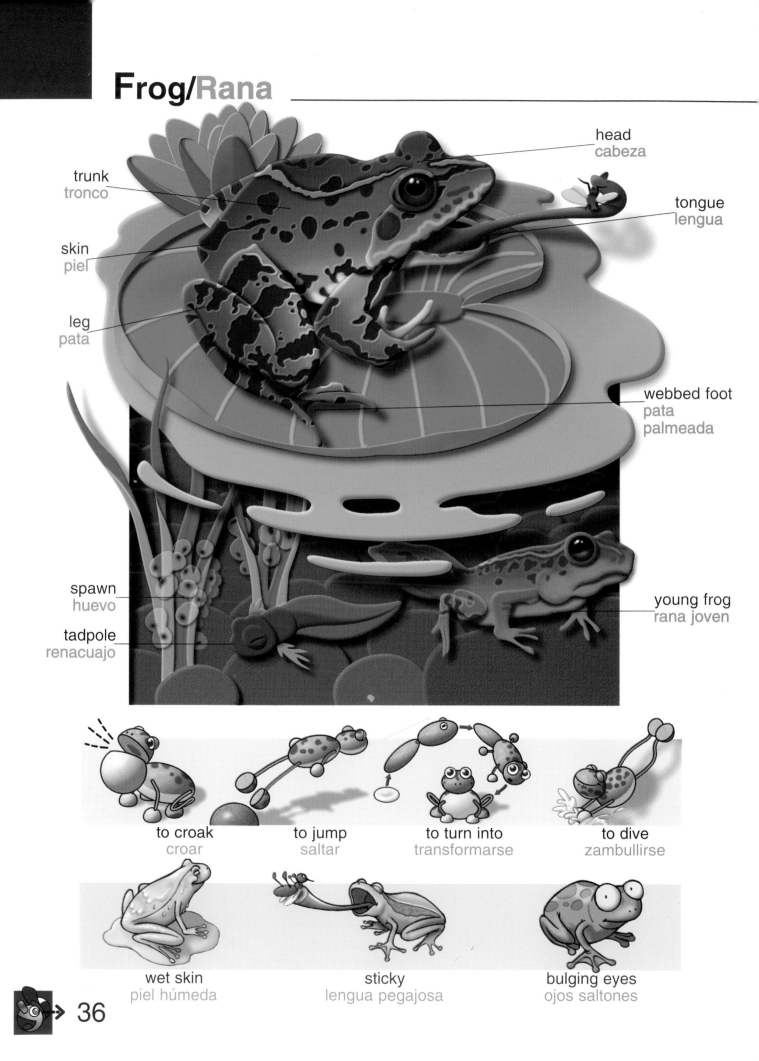

trunk
tronco

head
cabeza

tongue
lengua

skin
piel

leg
pata

webbed foot
pata
palmeada

spawn
huevo

tadpole
renacuajo

young frog
rana joven

to croak
croar

to jump
saltar

to turn into
transformarse

to dive
zambullirse

wet skin
piel húmeda

sticky
lengua pegajosa

bulging eyes
ojos saltones

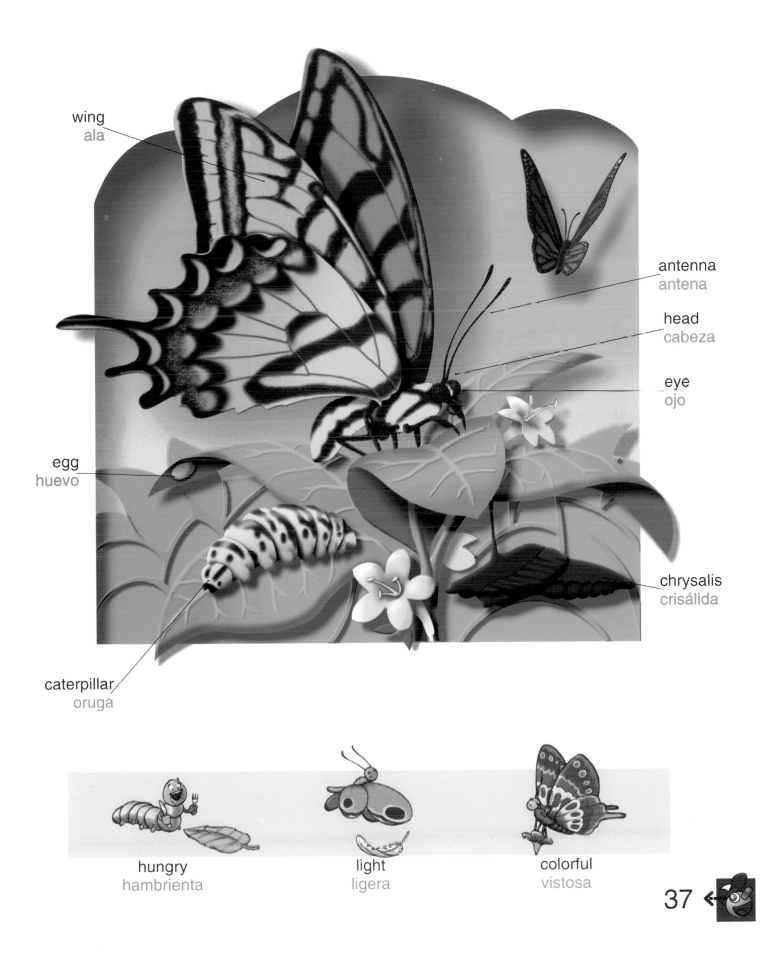

wing
ala

antenna
antena

head
cabeza

eye
ojo

egg
huevo

chrysalis
crisálida

caterpillar
oruga

hungry
hambrienta

light
ligera

colorful
vistosa

Bee/Abeja

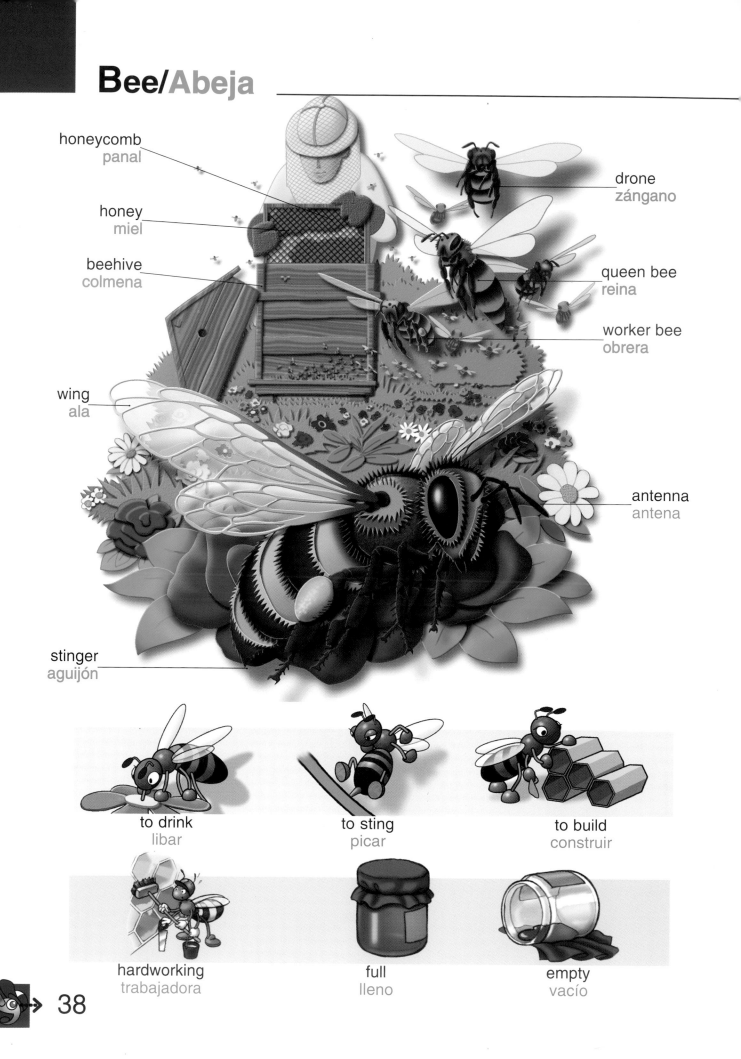

honeycomb
panal

honey
miel

beehive
colmena

wing
ala

stinger
aguijón

drone
zángano

queen bee
reina

worker bee
obrera

antenna
antena

to drink
libar

to sting
picar

to build
construir

hardworking
trabajadora

full
lleno

empty
vacío

Octopus and snail/Pulpo y caracol

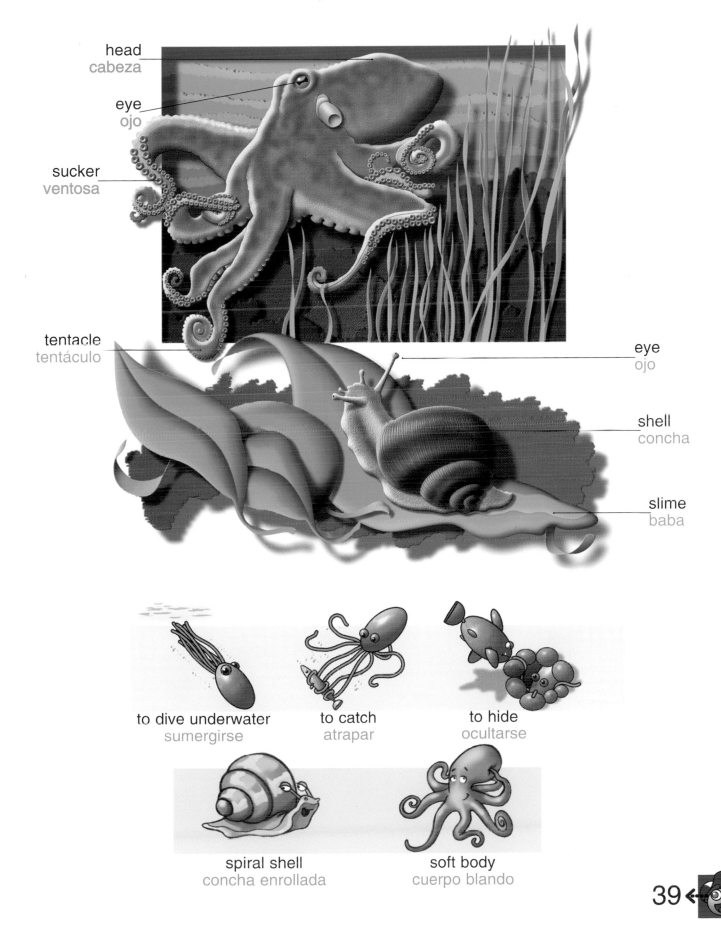

head
cabeza

eye
ojo

sucker
ventosa

tentacle
tentáculo

eye
ojo

shell
concha

slime
baba

to dive underwater
sumergirse

to catch
atrapar

to hide
ocultarse

spiral shell
concha enrollada

soft body
cuerpo blando

Other animals/Otros animales

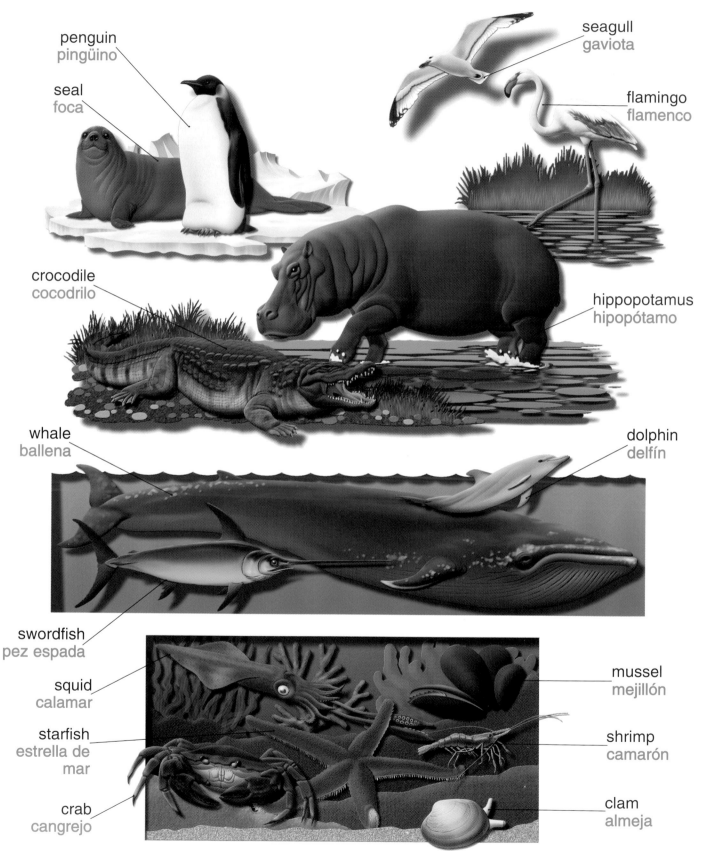

penguin
pingüino

seal
foca

seagull
gaviota

flamingo
flamenco

crocodile
cocodrilo

hippopotamus
hipopótamo

whale
ballena

dolphin
delfín

swordfish
pez espada

squid
calamar

mussel
mejillón

starfish
estrella de mar

shrimp
camarón

crab
cangrejo

clam
almeja

eagle
águila

giraffe
jirafa

gorilla
gorila

bear
oso

parrot
papagayo

kangaroo
canguro

zebra
cebra

elephant
elefante

wolf
lobo

ostrich
avestruz

wild boar
jabalí

hyena
hiena

leopard
leopardo

lion
león

tiger
tigre

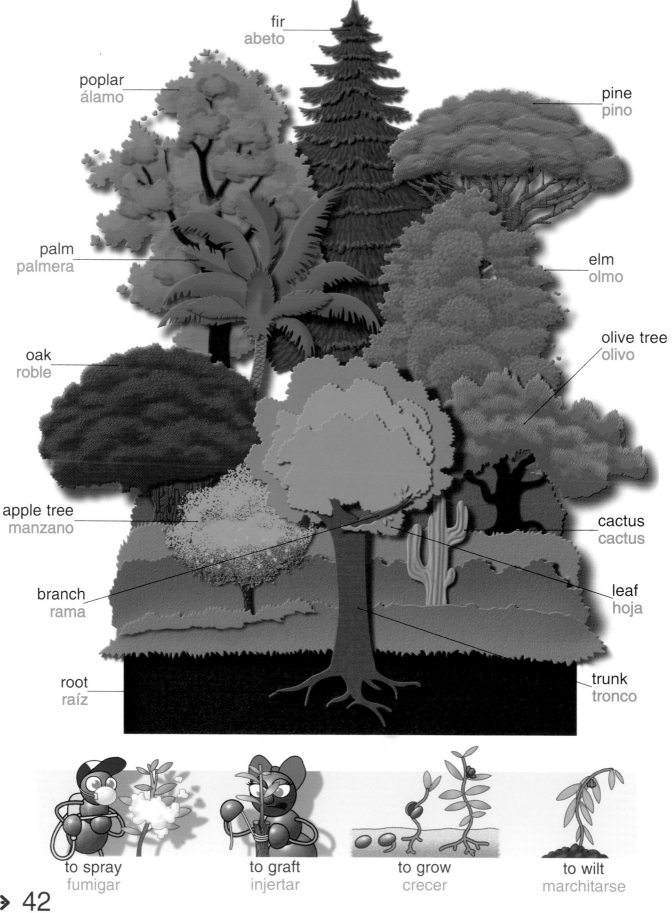

fir
abeto

poplar
álamo

pine
pino

palm
palmera

elm
olmo

olive tree
olivo

oak
roble

apple tree
manzano

cactus
cactus

branch
rama

leaf
hoja

root
raíz

trunk
tronco

to spray
fumigar

to graft
injertar

to grow
crecer

to wilt
marchitarse

petal
pétalo

carnation
clavel

rose
rosa

petunia
petunia

hydrangea
hortensia

chrysanthemum
crisantemo

pansy
pensamiento

hyacinth
jacinto

violet
violeta

stalk
tallo

daisy
margarita

dahlia
dalia

tulip
tulipán

lily
lirio

sweet smelling
perfumada

pretty
bonita

wilted
marchita

Fruit and nuts/Frutos

pineapple
piña

peach
durazno

grape
uva

plum
ciruela

custard apple
chirimoya

orange
naranja

cherry
cereza

fig
higo

tangerine
mandarina

walnut
nuez

hazelnut
avellana

date
dátil

pine nut
piñón

pistachio
pistacho

almond
almendra

peanut
cacahuate

watermelon
sandía

melon
melón

grapefruit
toronja

pear
pera

apricot
albaricoque

banana
plátano

lemon
limón

apple
manzana

strawberry
fresa

kiwi
kiwi

raspberry
frambuesa

unripe
verde

ripe
madura

rotten
podrida

44

Vegetables, legumes, and cereals
Verduras, legumbres y cereales

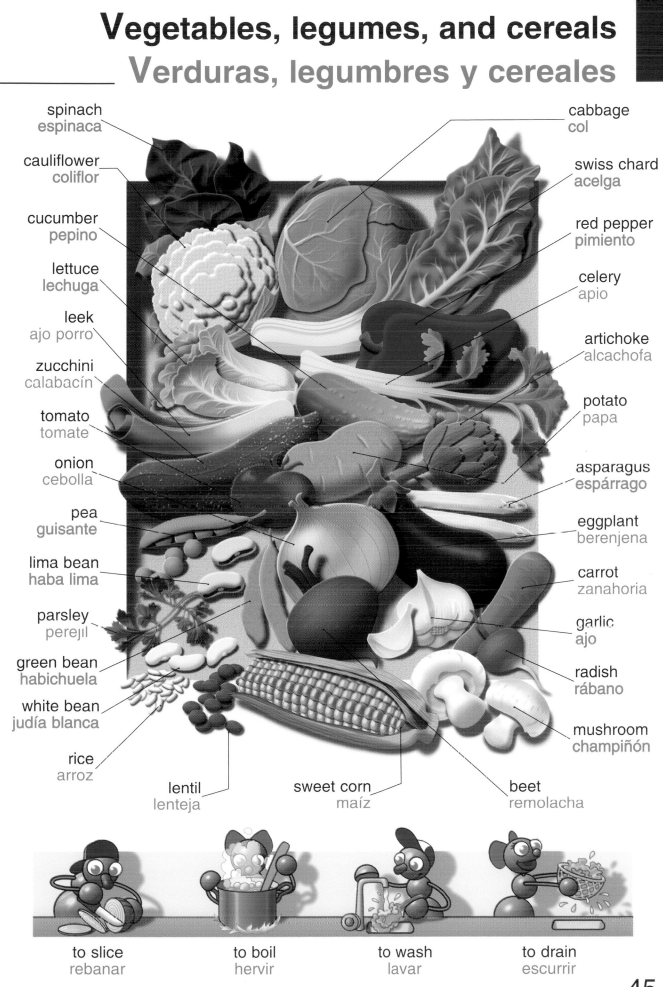

spinach
espinaca

cauliflower
coliflor

cucumber
pepino

lettuce
lechuga

leek
ajo porro

zucchini
calabacín

tomato
tomate

onion
cebolla

pea
guisante

lima bean
haba lima

parsley
perejil

green bean
habichuela

white bean
judía blanca

rice
arroz

cabbage
col

swiss chard
acelga

red pepper
pimiento

celery
apio

artichoke
alcachofa

potato
papa

asparagus
espárrago

eggplant
berenjena

carrot
zanahoria

garlic
ajo

radish
rábano

mushroom
champiñón

lentil
lenteja

sweet corn
maíz

beet
remolacha

to slice
rebanar

to boil
hervir

to wash
lavar

to drain
escurrir

Garden/Jardín

greenhouse
invernadero

toolshed
cobertizo

fence
cerca

flower bed
jardín de flores

hedge
seto

flower
flor

seed
semilla

grass
hierba

soil
tierra

gardener
jardinero

path
camino

tidy
cuidado

untidy
descuidado

trimmed
recortado

Garden tools/Herramientas de jardín

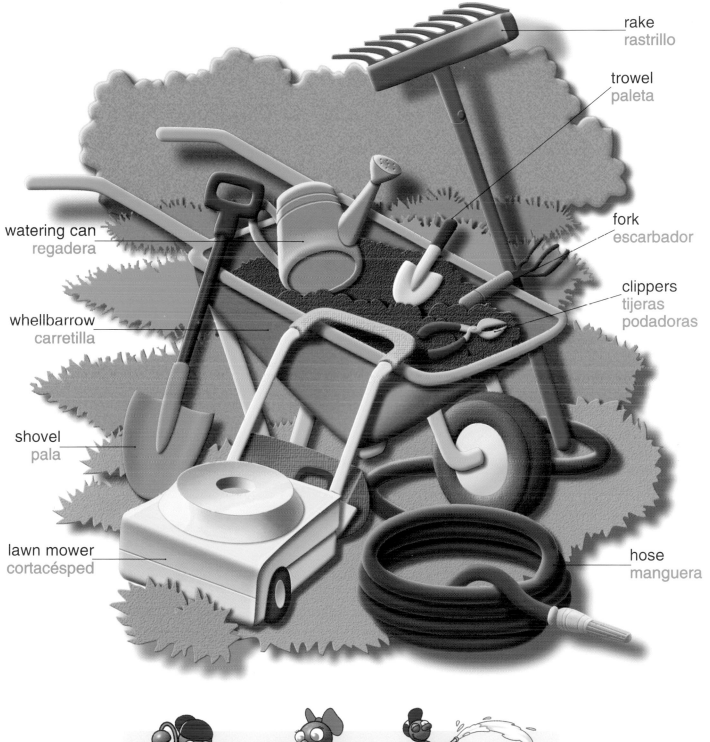

rake
rastrillo

trowel
paleta

fork
escarbador

clippers
tijeras
podadoras

watering can
regadera

whellbarrow
carretilla

shovel
pala

lawn mower
cortacésped

hose
manguera

to dig
cavar

to plant
plantar

to water
regar

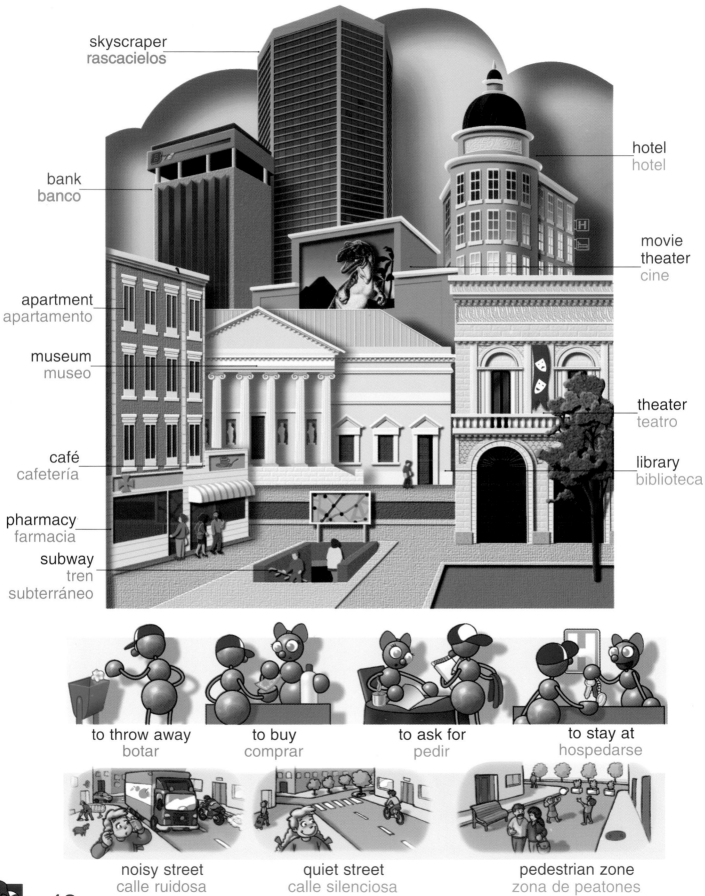

skyscraper
rascacielos

bank
banco

apartment
apartamento

museum
museo

café
cafetería

pharmacy
farmacia

subway
tren
subterráneo

hotel
hotel

movie theater
cine

theater
teatro

library
biblioteca

to throw away
botar

to buy
comprar

to ask for
pedir

to stay at
hospedarse

noisy street
calle ruidosa

quiet street
calle silenciosa

pedestrian zone
zona de peatones

A city street/Una calle de la ciudad

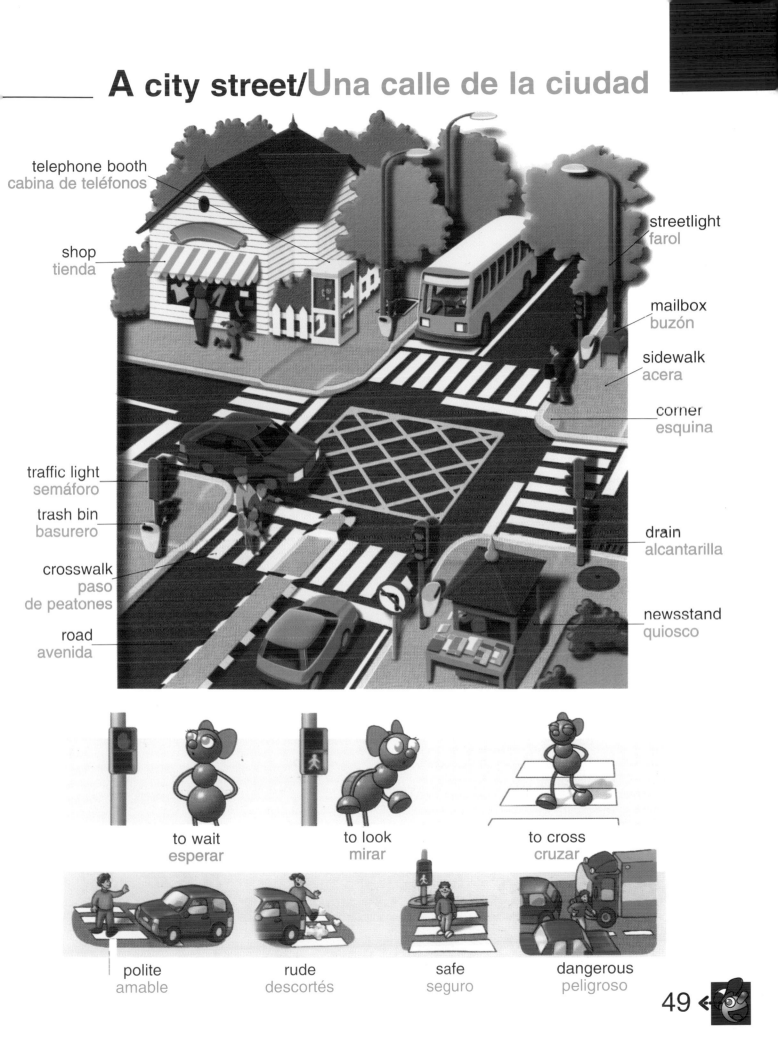

telephone booth
cabina de teléfonos

shop
tienda

streetlight
farol

mailbox
buzón

sidewalk
acera

corner
esquina

traffic light
semáforo

trash bin
basurero

drain
alcantarilla

crosswalk
paso
de peatones

newsstand
quiosco

road
avenida

to wait
esperar

to look
mirar

to cross
cruzar

polite
amable

rude
descortés

safe
seguro

dangerous
peligroso

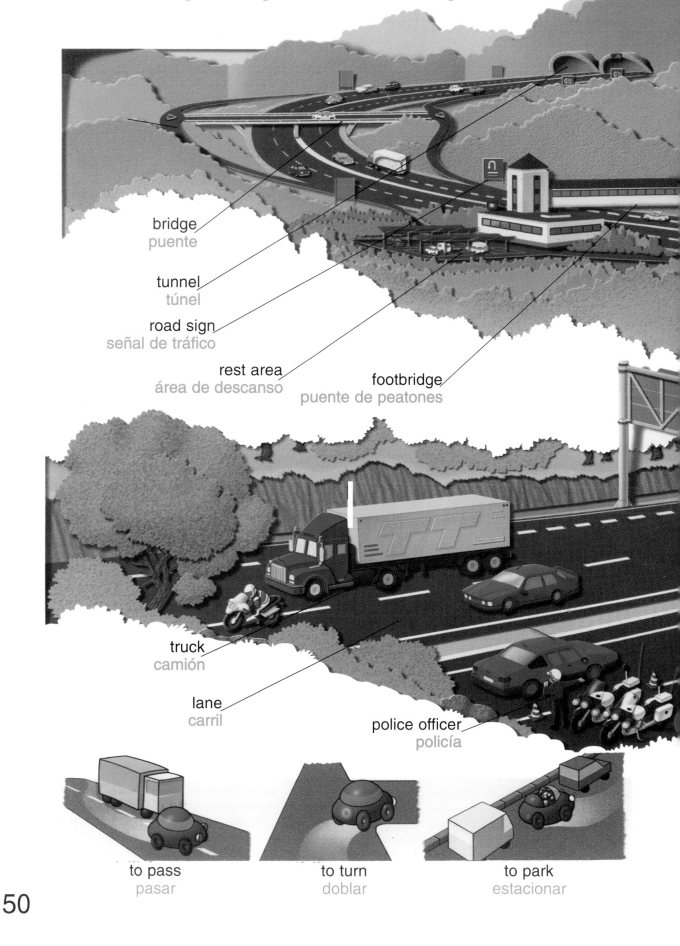

bridge
puente

tunnel
túnel

road sign
señal de tráfico

rest area
área de descanso

footbridge
puente de peatones

truck
camión

lane
carril

police officer
policía

to pass
pasar

to turn
doblar

to park
estacionar

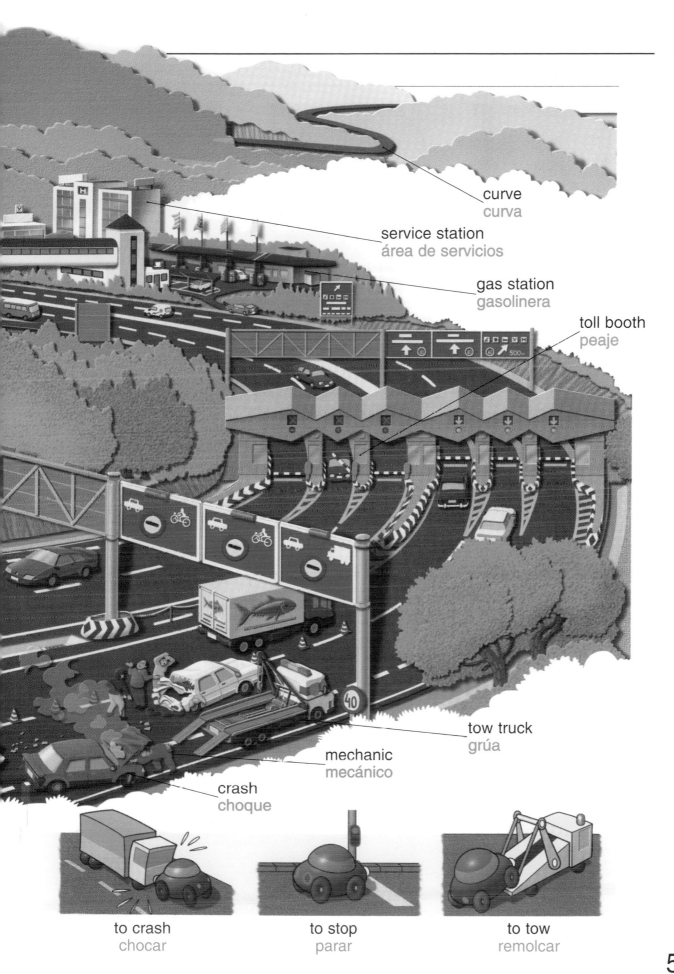

curve
curva

service station
área de servicios

gas station
gasolinera

toll booth
peaje

tow truck
grúa

mechanic
mecánico

crash
choque

to crash
chocar

to stop
parar

to tow
remolcar

JOBS/LOS TRABAJOS
Some jobs/Algunos trabajos

plumber
plomero

teacher
profesor

veterinarian
veterinaria

bricklayer
albañil

lawyer
abogada

fishdealer
pescadera

butcher
carnicero

electrician
electricista

grocer
frutera

to bandage
vendar

to work
trabajar

to rest
descansar

to weigh
pesar

More jobs/Otros trabajos

pharmacist
farmacéutica

fisher
pescador

painter
pintor

farmer
agricultor

reporter
periodista

taxi driver
taxista

barber/hairdresser
barbero/peluquero

photographer
fotógrafa

model
modelo

to teach
enseñar

to fish
pescar

to cut
cortar

to take photos
fotografiar

53

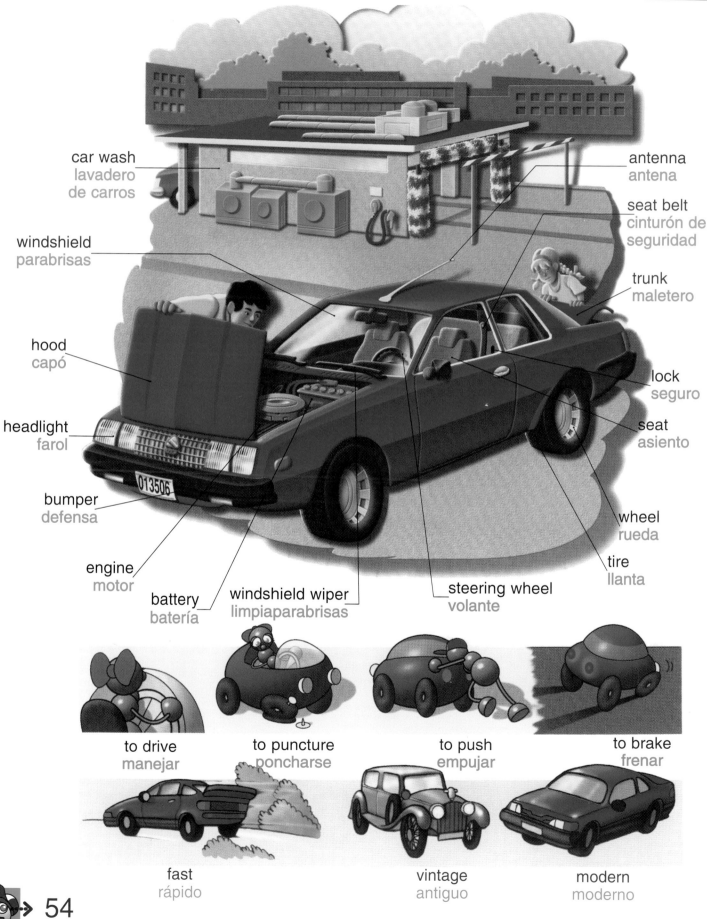

car wash
lavadero
de carros

antenna
antena

seat belt
cinturón de
seguridad

windshield
parabrisas

trunk
maletero

hood
capó

lock
seguro

headlight
farol

seat
asiento

bumper
defensa

wheel
rueda

engine
motor

tire
llanta

battery
batería

windshield wiper
limpiaparabrisas

steering wheel
volante

to drive
manejar

to puncture
poncharse

to push
empujar

to brake
frenar

fast
rápido

vintage
antiguo

modern
moderno

Bicycle and motorcycle/Bicicleta y moto

seat
asiento

mirror
espejo retrovisor

brake
freno

exhaust pipe
tubo de escape

motor
motor

helmet
casco

bell
timbre

wheel
goma

handlebars
manubrio

seat
asiento

pedal
pedal

chain
cadena

to pedal
pedalear

to pump up
inflar

to oil
engrasar

to stop
detenerse

deflated
desinflada

big
grande

medium-sized
mediana

small
pequeña

55

At the station/La estación de tren

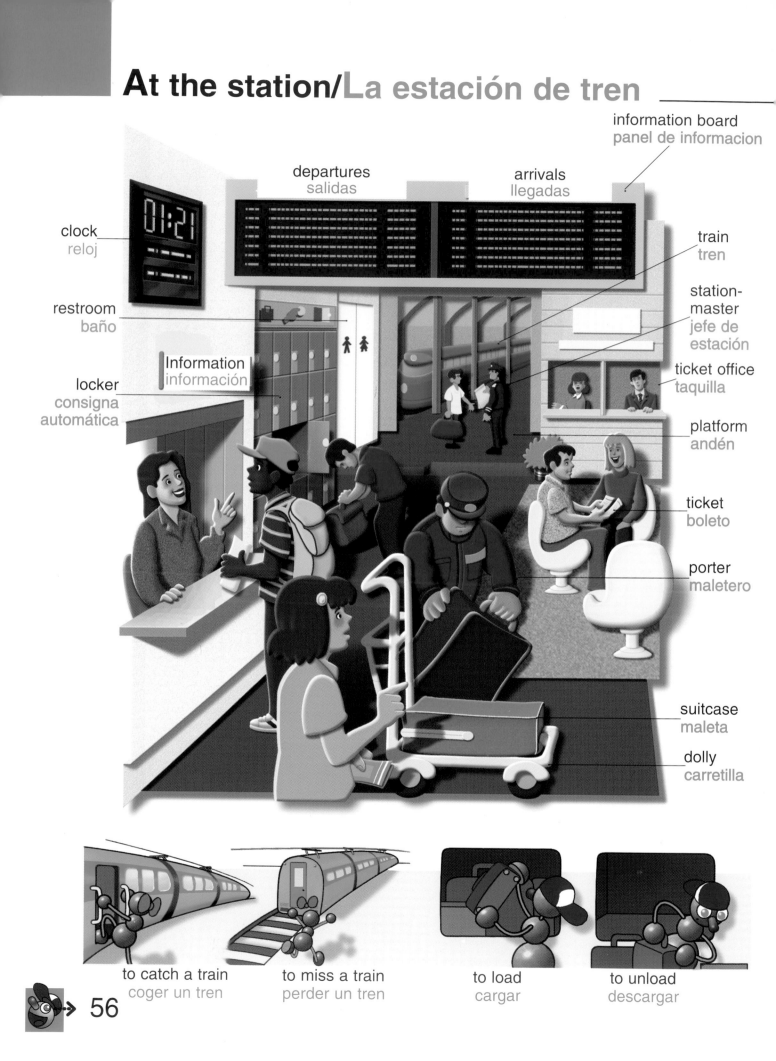

information board
panel de informacion

departures
salidas

arrivals
llegadas

clock
reloj

train
tren

station-master
jefe de estación

restroom
baño

Information
información

ticket office
taquilla

locker
consigna automática

platform
andén

ticket
boleto

porter
maletero

suitcase
maleta

dolly
carretilla

to catch a train
coger un tren

to miss a train
perder un tren

to load
cargar

to unload
descargar

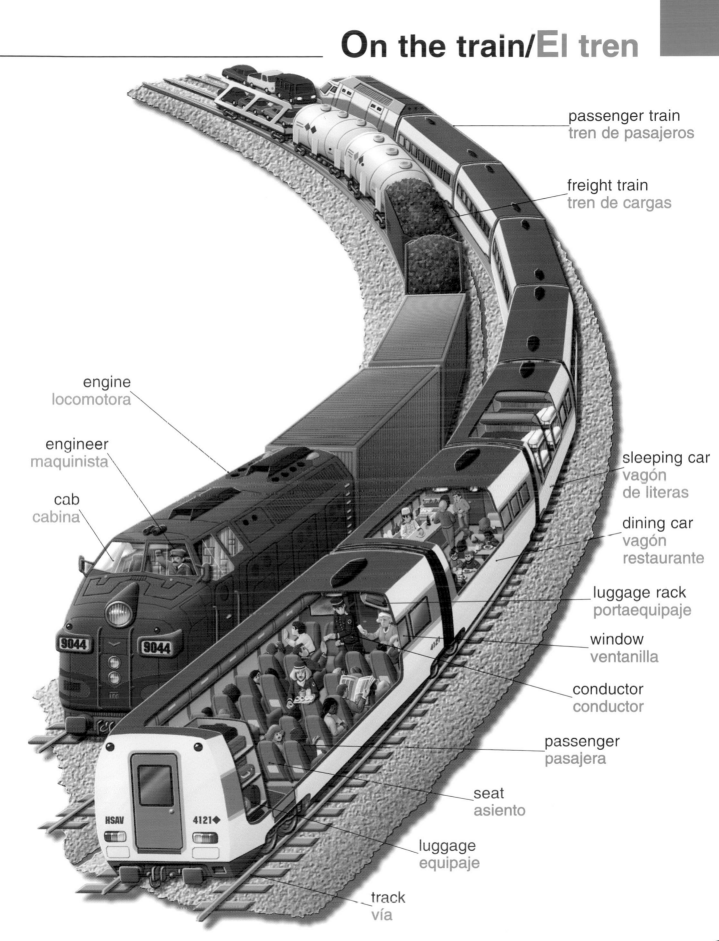

passenger train
tren de pasajeros

freight train
tren de cargas

engine
locomotora

engineer
maquinista

cab
cabina

sleeping car
vagón
de literas

dining car
vagón
restaurante

luggage rack
portaequipaje

window
ventanilla

conductor
conductor

passenger
pasajera

seat
asiento

luggage
equipaje

track
vía

9044   9044

HSAV   4121◆

57

At the airport/El aeropuerto

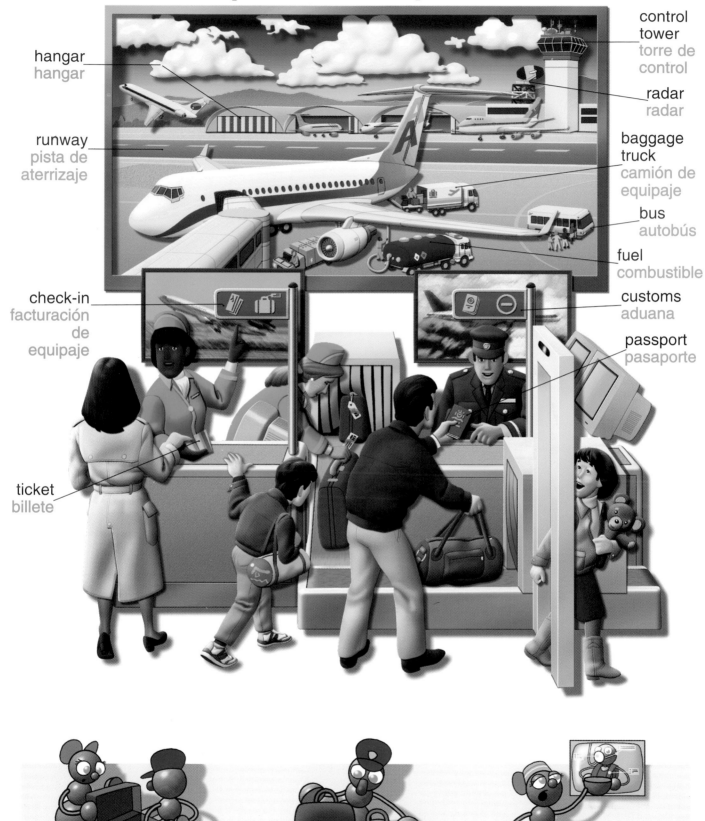

hangar
hangar

runway
pista de
aterrizaje

control
tower
torre de
control

radar
radar

baggage
truck
camión de
equipaje

bus
autobús

fuel
combustible

check-in
facturación
de
equipaje

customs
aduana

passport
pasaporte

ticket
billete

to show
enseñar

to inspect
inspeccionar

to explain
explicar

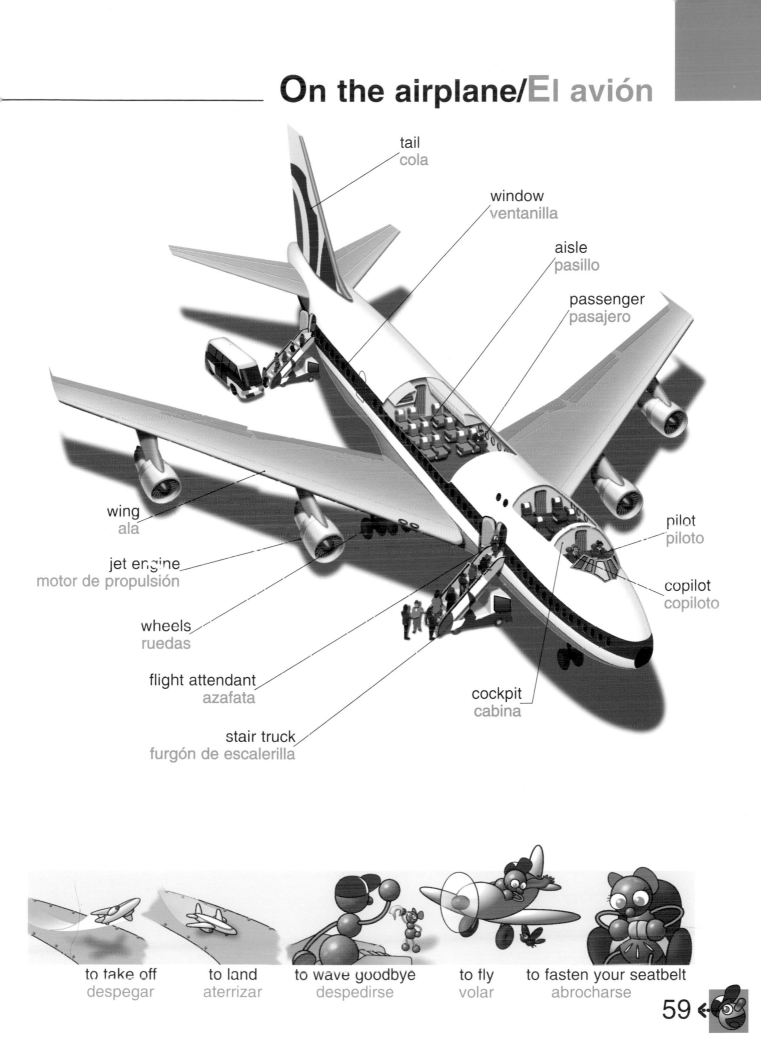

tail
cola

window
ventanilla

aisle
pasillo

passenger
pasajero

wing
ala

jet engine
motor de propulsión

wheels
ruedas

flight attendant
azafata

stair truck
furgón de escalerilla

pilot
piloto

copilot
copiloto

cockpit
cabina

to take off
despegar

to land
aterrizar

to wave goodbye
despedirse

to fly
volar

to fasten your seatbelt
abrocharse

59

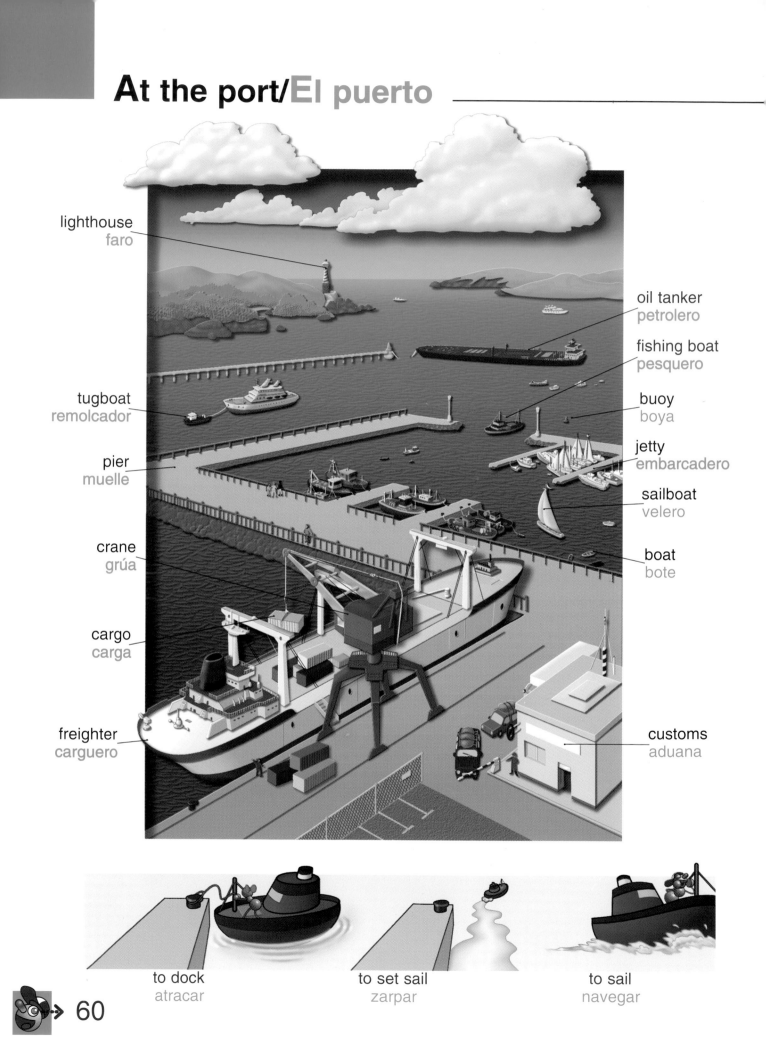

lighthouse
faro

oil tanker
petrolero

fishing boat
pesquero

tugboat
remolcador

buoy
boya

pier
muelle

jetty
embarcadero

sailboat
velero

crane
grúa

boat
bote

cargo
carga

freighter
carguero

customs
aduana

to dock
atracar

to set sail
zarpar

to sail
navegar

On a ship/El barco

deck
cubierta

funnel
chimenea

lifeboat
bote salvavidas

porthole
claraboya

radar
radar

anchor
ancla

prow
proa

stern
popa

rudder
timón

propeller
hélice

engine room
sala de máquinas

cargo hold
bodega

cabin
camarote

to embark
embarcar

to disembark
desembarcar

to float
flotar

to sink
hundirse

kite
papalote

skate-
board
mono-
patín

roller
skates
patines
de ruedas

hide
-and-
seek
escondite

slide
canal

swing
columpio

seesaw
subibaja

jump
rope
cuerda
de saltar

tricycle
triciclo

marbles
canicas

to swing
columpiarse

to skate
patinar

to climb
trepar

to go down
lanzarse

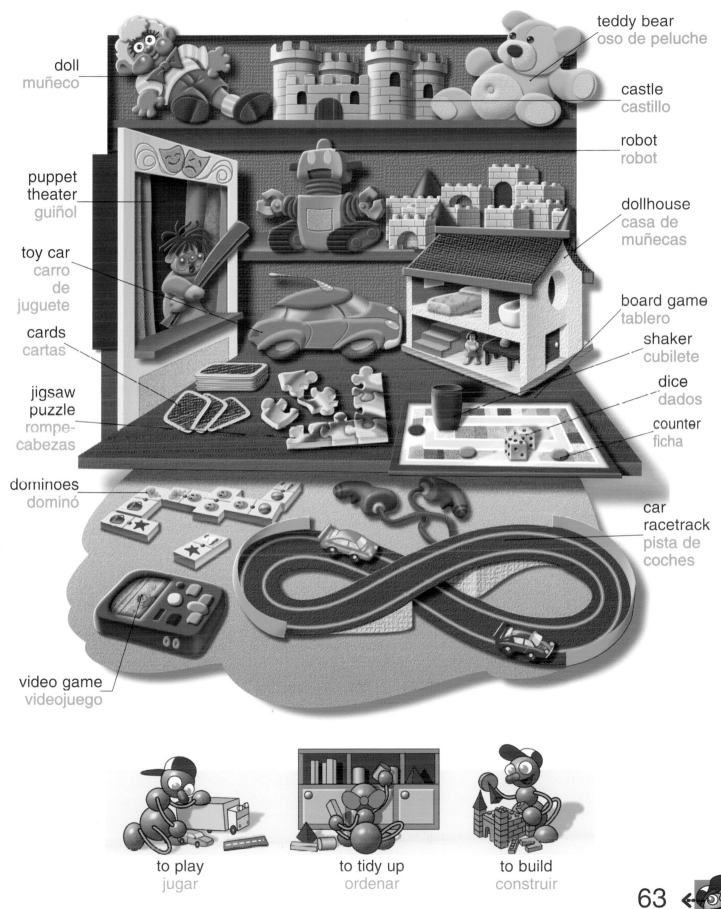

teddy bear
oso de peluche

doll
muñeco

castle
castillo

robot
robot

puppet
theater
guiñol

dollhouse
casa de
muñecas

toy car
carro
de
juguete

board game
tablero

shaker
cubilete

cards
cartas

dice
dados

jigsaw
puzzle
rompe-
cabezas

counter
ficha

dominoes
dominó

car
racetrack
pista de
coches

video game
videojuego

to play
jugar

to tidy up
ordenar

to build
construir

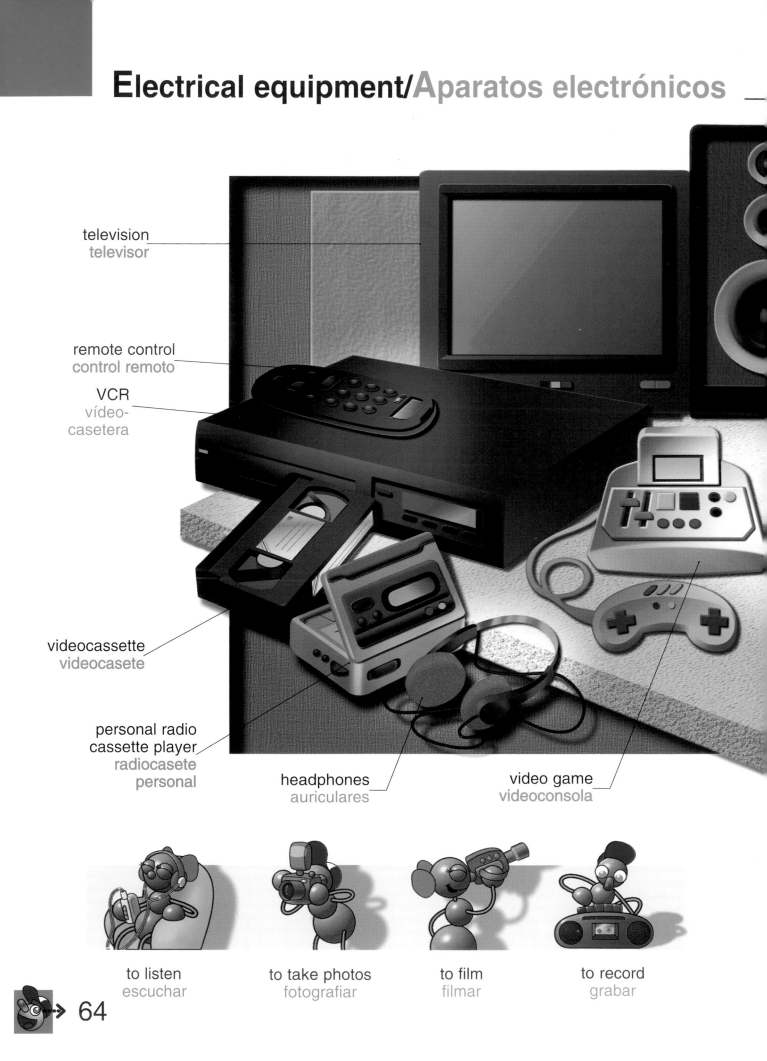

television
televisor

remote control
control remoto

VCR
vídeo-
casetera

videocassette
videocasete

personal radio
cassette player
radiocasete
personal

headphones
auriculares

video game
videoconsola

to listen
escuchar

to take photos
fotografiar

to film
filmar

to record
grabar

64

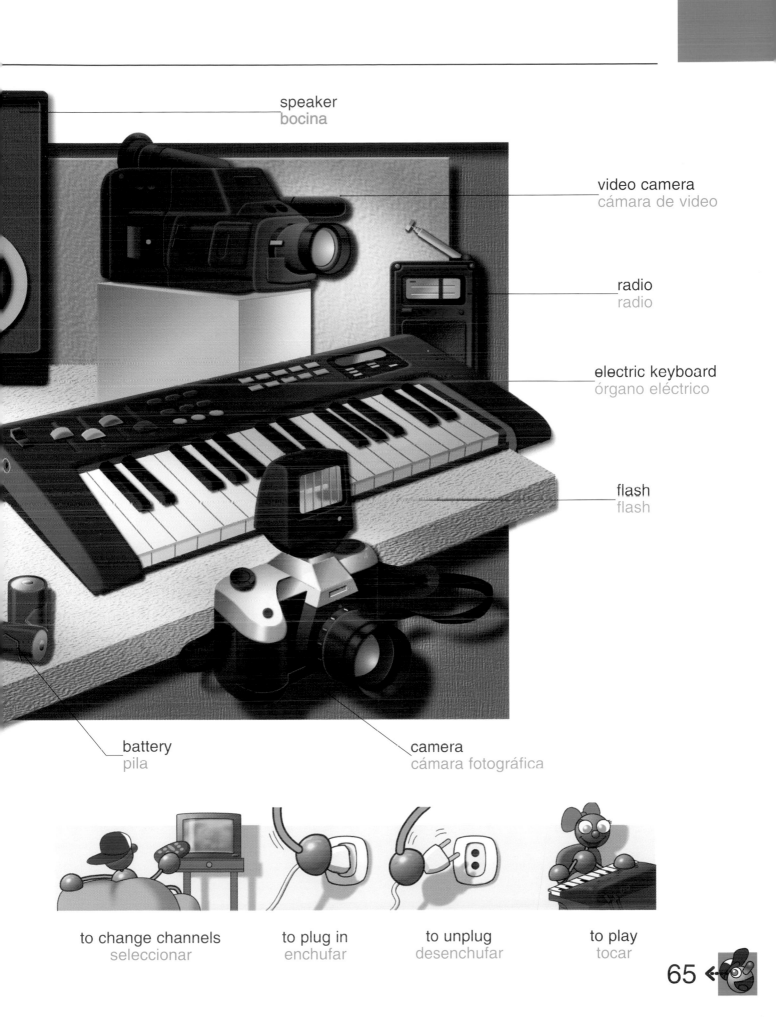

speaker
bocina

video camera
cámara de video

radio
radio

electric keyboard
órgano eléctrico

flash
flash

battery
pila

camera
cámara fotográfica

to change channels
seleccionar

to plug in
enchufar

to unplug
desenchufar

to play
tocar

At a theater/El cine y el teatro

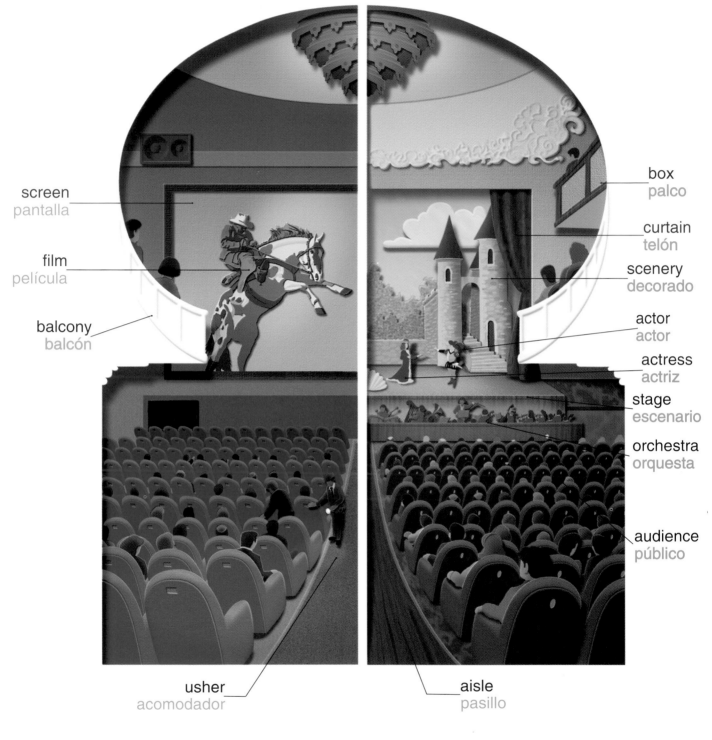

screen
pantalla

film
película

balcony
balcón

box
palco

curtain
telón

scenery
decorado

actor
actor

actress
actriz

stage
escenario

orchestra
orquesta

audience
público

usher
acomodador

aisle
pasillo

to cry
llorar

to laugh
reír

to applaud
aplaudir

to go in
entrar

to come out
salir

In the television studio/El estudio de televisión

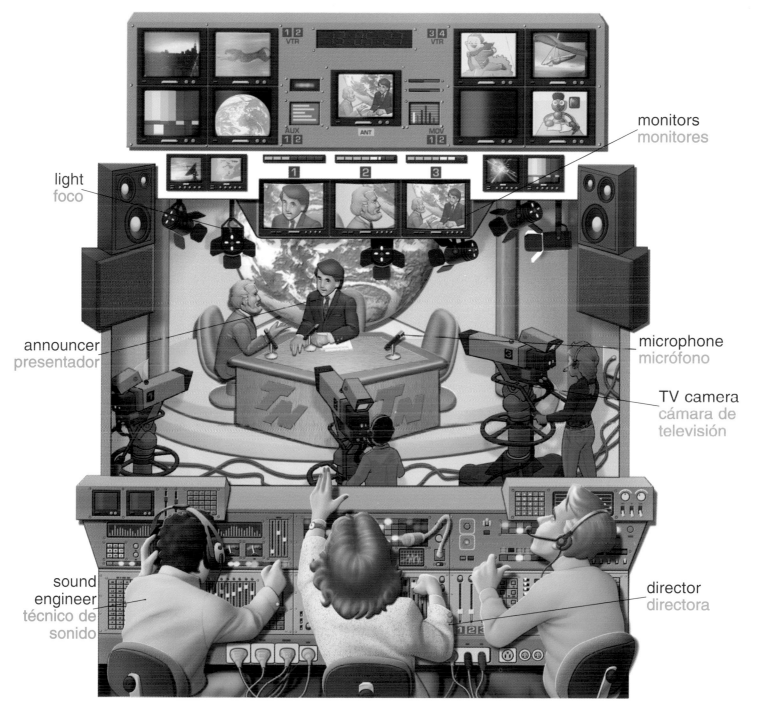

monitors
monitores

light
foco

announcer
presentador

microphone
micrófono

TV camera
cámara de televisión

sound engineer
técnico de sonido

director
directora

to put on makeup
maquillar

to announce
presentar

to direct
dirigir

Musical instruments/Instrumentos musicales

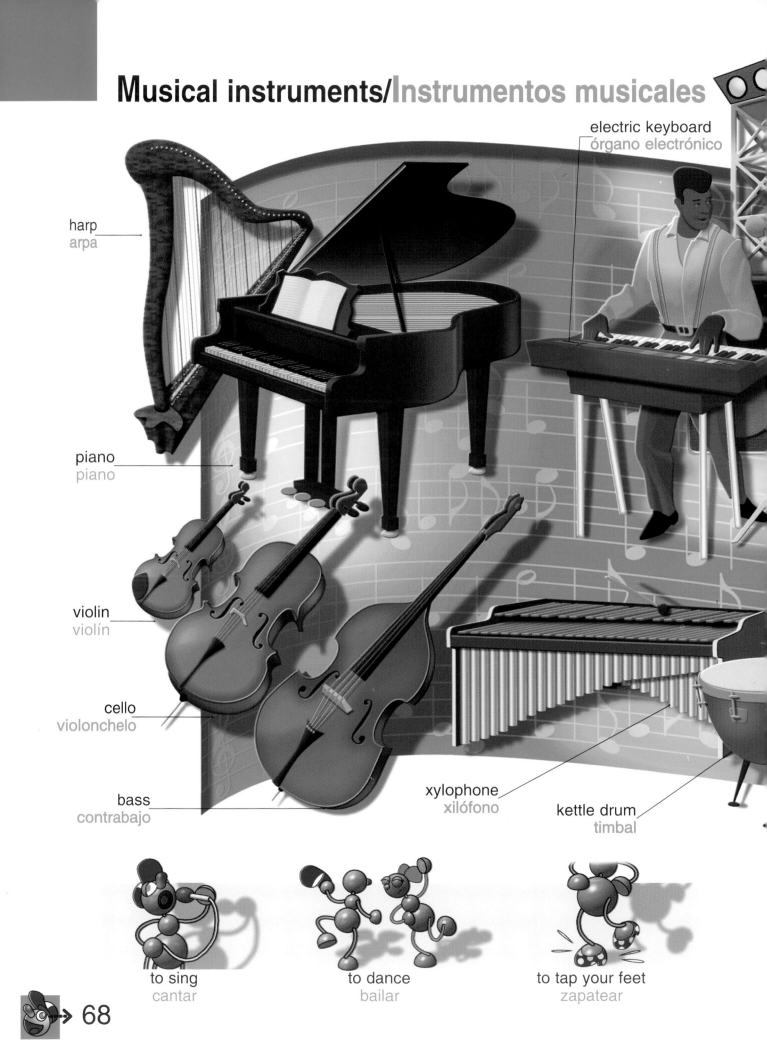

electric keyboard
órgano electrónico

harp
arpa

piano
piano

violin
violín

cello
violonchelo

bass
contrabajo

xylophone
xilófono

kettle drum
timbal

to sing
cantar

to dance
bailar

to tap your feet
zapatear

electric guitar
guitarra eléctrica

drum set
batería

amplifier
amplificador

saxophone
saxofón

trumpet
trompeta

trombone
trombón

flute
flauta

clarinet
clarinete

castanets
castañuelas

maraca
maraca

drum
tambor

cymbal
platillo

tambourine
pandereta

to strum
rasguear

to shake
sacudir

to blow
soplar

69

Sports/Los deportes
Basketball/Baloncesto

player
jugadora

ball
pelota

hoop
aro

backboard
tablero

net
canasta

substitute
suplente

referee
árbitro

umpire
juez

bench
banco

knee pad
rodillera

athletic shoe
zapato
deportivo

to dribble
driblar

to push
empujar

to score
colar la pelota

to pass
pasar

tall
alta

short
bajita

tired
fatigada

SOCCER/Fútbol

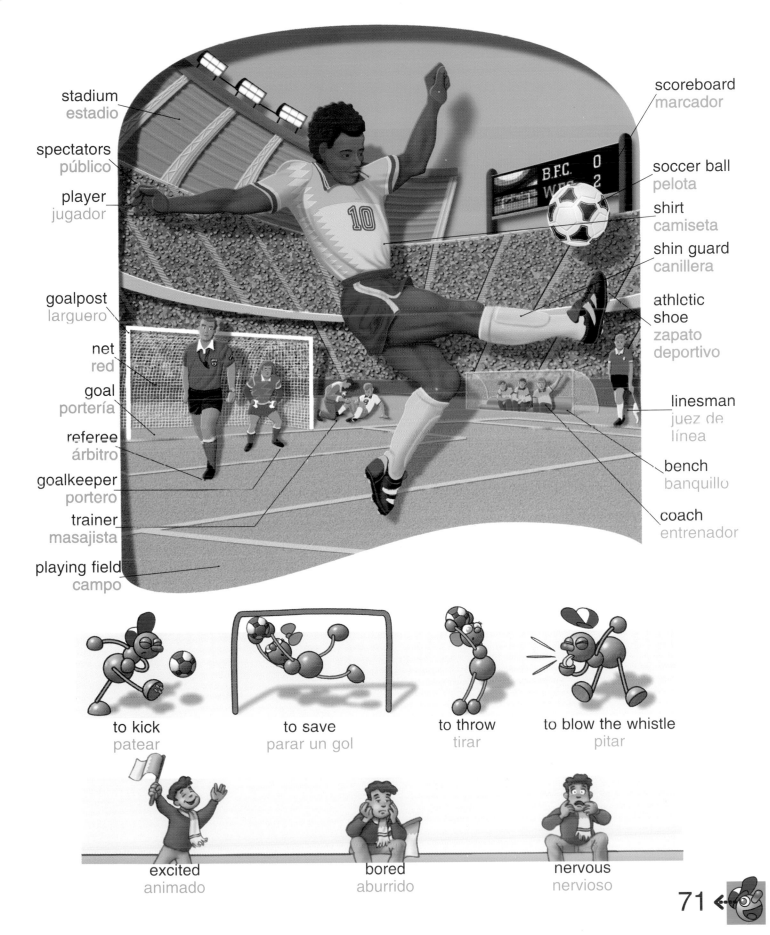

stadium
estadio

spectators
público

player
jugador

goalpost
larguero

net
red

goal
portería

referee
árbitro

goalkeeper
portero

trainer
masajista

playing field
campo

scoreboard
marcador

soccer ball
pelota

shirt
camiseta

shin guard
canillera

athlctic
shoe
zapato
deportivo

linesman
juez de
línea

bench
banquillo

coach
entrenador

B.F.C. 0
W.F.C. 2

to kick
patear

to save
parar un gol

to throw
tirar

to blow the whistle
pitar

excited
animado

bored
aburrido

nervous
nervioso

Tennis/Tenis

player
tenista

raquet
raqueta

wristband
muñequera

line
judge
juez
de línea

ball
pelota

net
red

court
cancha

to serve
lanzar

to return
devolver

to hit
golpear

Swimming/Natación

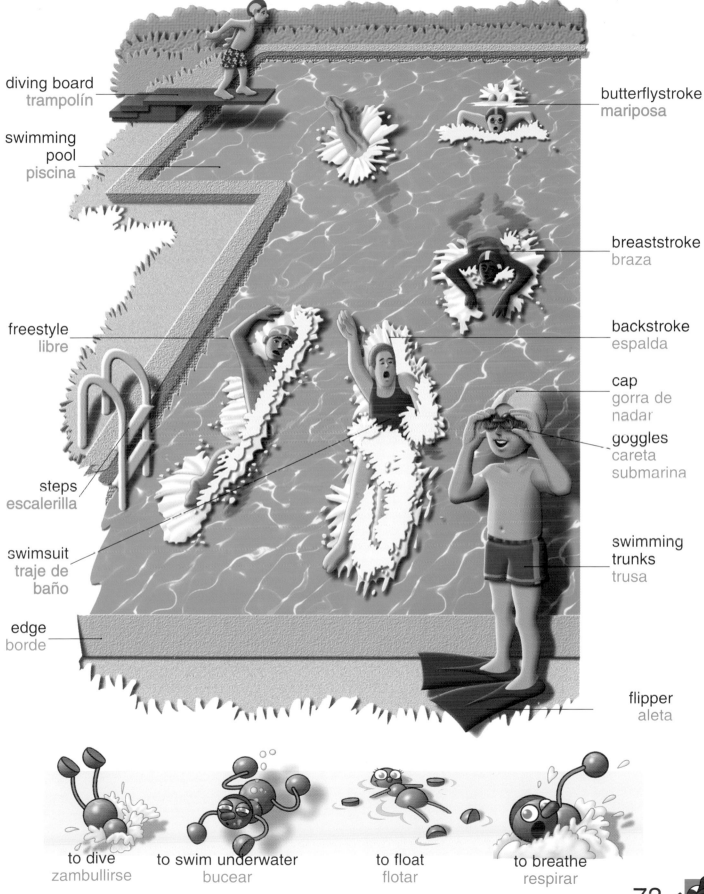

diving board
trampolín

swimming pool
piscina

freestyle
libre

steps
escalerilla

swimsuit
traje de baño

edge
borde

butterflystroke
mariposa

breaststroke
braza

backstroke
espalda

cap
gorra de nadar

goggles
careta submarina

swimming trunks
trusa

flipper
aleta

to dive
zambullirse

to swim underwater
bucear

to float
flotar

to breathe
respirar

Skiing/Esquí

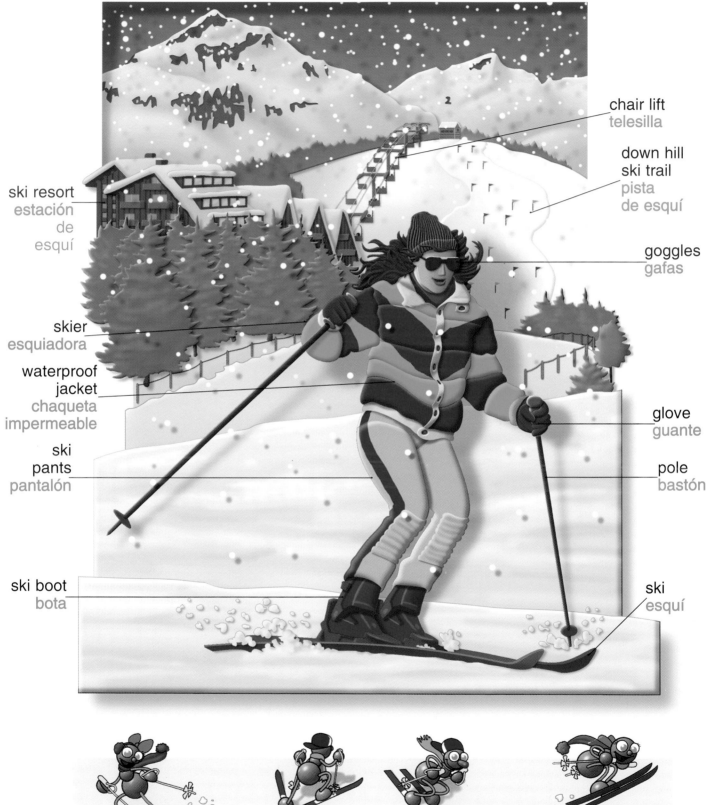

chair lift
telesilla

down hill
ski trail
pista
de esquí

ski resort
estación
de
esquí

goggles
gafas

skier
esquiadora

waterproof
jacket
chaqueta
impermeable

glove
guante

ski
pants
pantalón

pole
bastón

ski boot
bota

ski
esquí

to ski
esquiar

to go up
ascender

to go down
descender

to jump
saltar

Gymnastics and athletics/Gimnasia y atletismo

pole vault
salto con garrocha

high jump
salto de altura

bar
barra

hoop
aro

runner
corredor

running track
pista para
carreras

horse
potro

parallel bars
paralelas

mat
colchoneta

to jump
saltar

to run
correr

to swing
balancearse

to go through
pasar

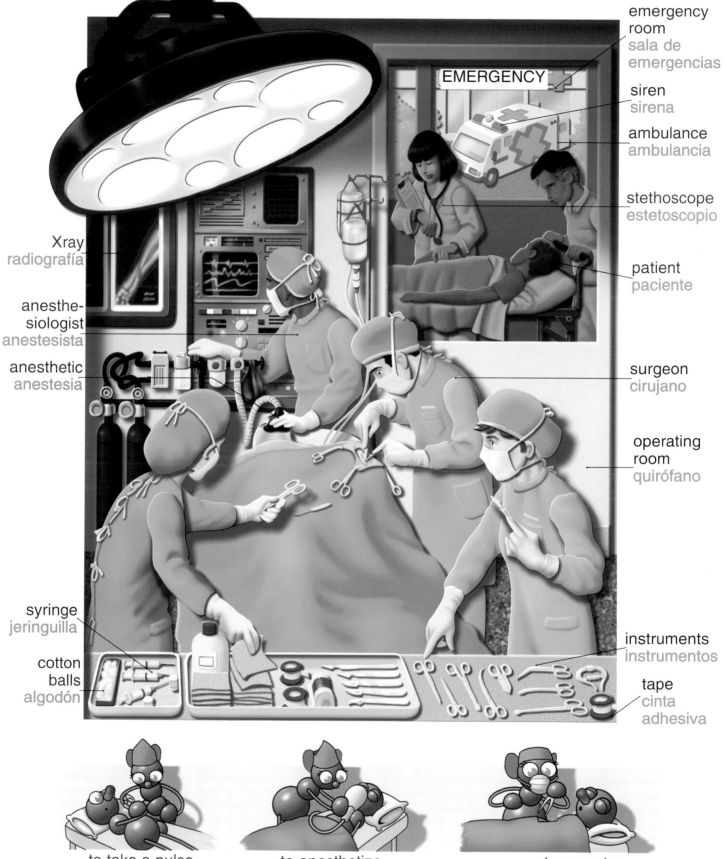

emergency room
sala de emergencias

siren
sirena

ambulance
ambulancia

stethoscope
estetoscopio

patient
paciente

surgeon
cirujano

operating room
quirófano

instruments
instrumentos

tape
cinta adhesiva

Xray
radiografía

anesthe-siologist
anestesista

anesthetic
anestesia

syringe
jeringuilla

cotton balls
algodón

EMERGENCY

to take a pulse
tomar el pulso

to anesthetize
anestesiar

to operate
operar

Fire station/Estación de bomberos

fire engine
bomba de incendios

ladder
escalera

helmet
casco

alarm
alarma

firefighter
bombero

hose
manguera

to rescue
rescatar

to feel dizzy
marearse

to put out
apagar

Post office/Oficina de correos

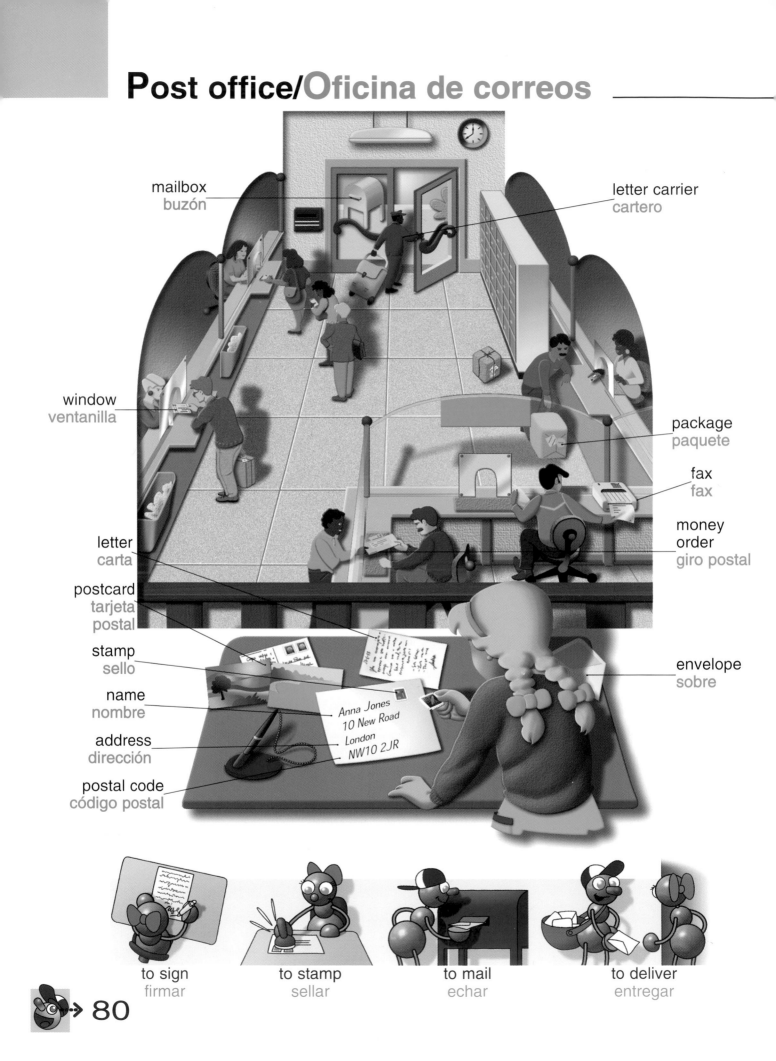

mailbox
buzón

letter carrier
cartero

window
ventanilla

package
paquete

fax
fax

letter
carta

money
order
giro postal

postcard
tarjeta
postal

stamp
sello

envelope
sobre

name
nombre

Anna Jones
10 New Road
London
NW10 2JR

address
dirección

postal code
código postal

to sign
firmar

to stamp
sellar

to mail
echar

to deliver
entregar

Supermarket/Supermercado

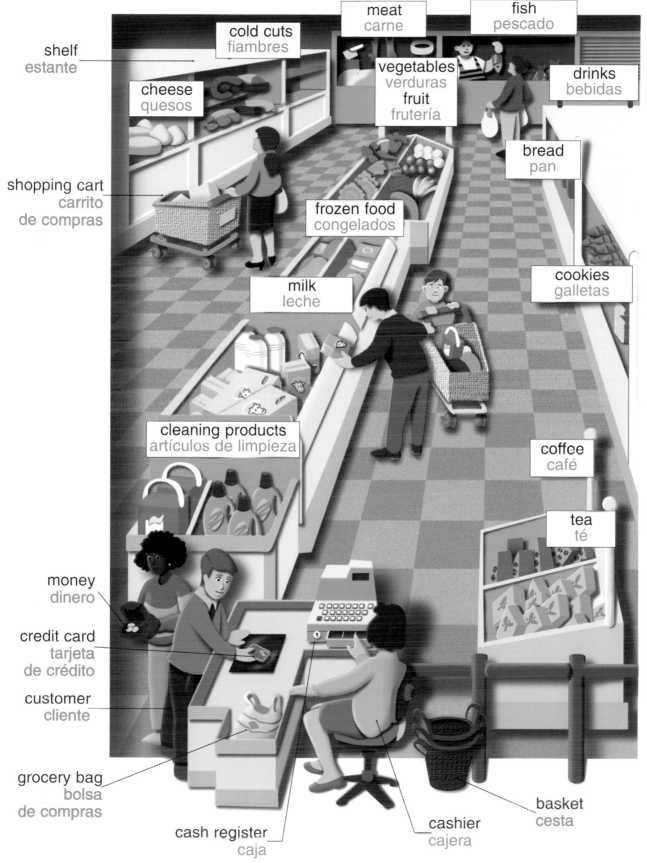

shelf
estante

cold cuts
fiambres

meat
carne

fish
pescado

cheese
quesos

vegetables
verduras
fruit
frutería

drinks
bebidas

shopping cart
carrito
de compras

bread
pan

frozen food
congelados

milk
leche

cookies
galletas

cleaning products
artículos de limpieza

coffee
café

tea
té

money
dinero

credit card
tarjeta
de crédito

customer
cliente

grocery bag
bolsa
de compras

basket
cesta

cash register
caja

cashier
cajera

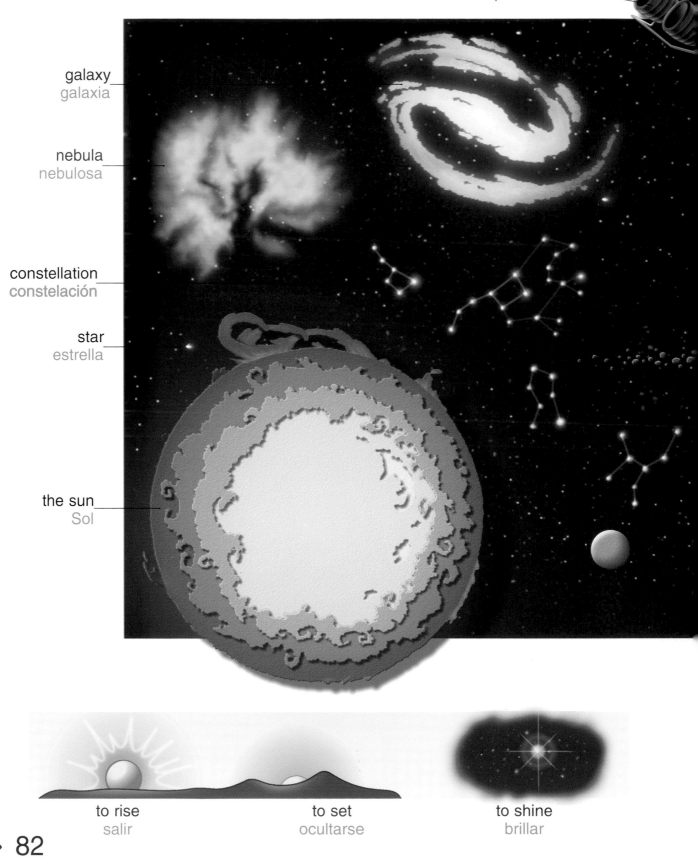

spaceship
nave espacial

galaxy
galaxia

nebula
nebulosa

constellation
constelación

star
estrella

the sun
Sol

to rise
salir

to set
ocultarse

to shine
brillar

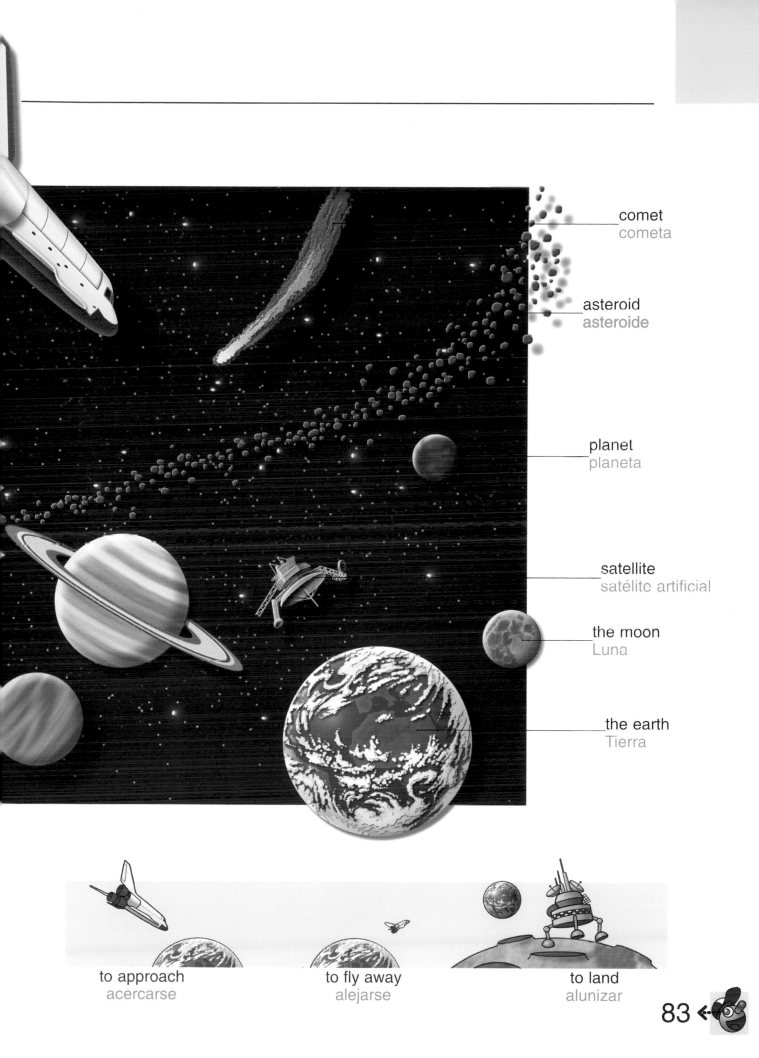

comet
cometa

asteroid
asteroide

planet
planeta

satellite
satélite artificial

the moon
Luna

the earth
Tierra

to approach
acercarse

to fly away
alejarse

to land
alunizar

In the country/El campo

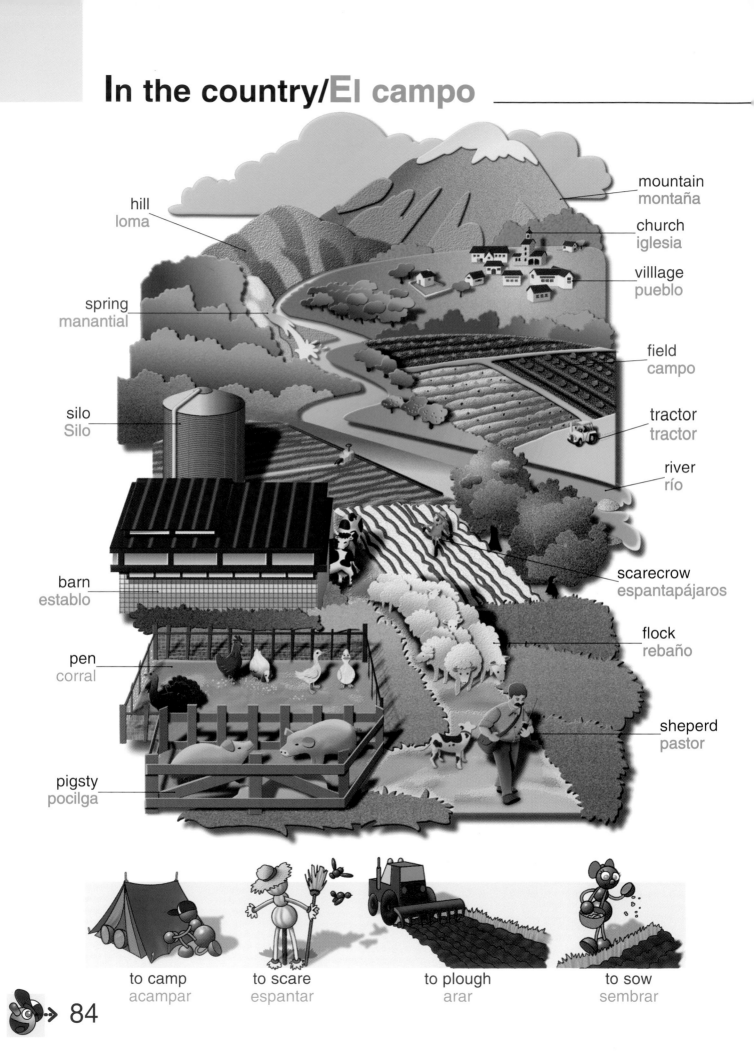

hill
loma

mountain
montaña

church
iglesia

villlage
pueblo

spring
manantial

field
campo

silo
Silo

tractor
tractor

river
río

barn
establo

scarecrow
espantapájaros

flock
rebaño

pen
corral

sheperd
pastor

pigsty
pocilga

to camp
acampar

to scare
espantar

to plough
arar

to sow
sembrar

On the beach/La playa y el mar

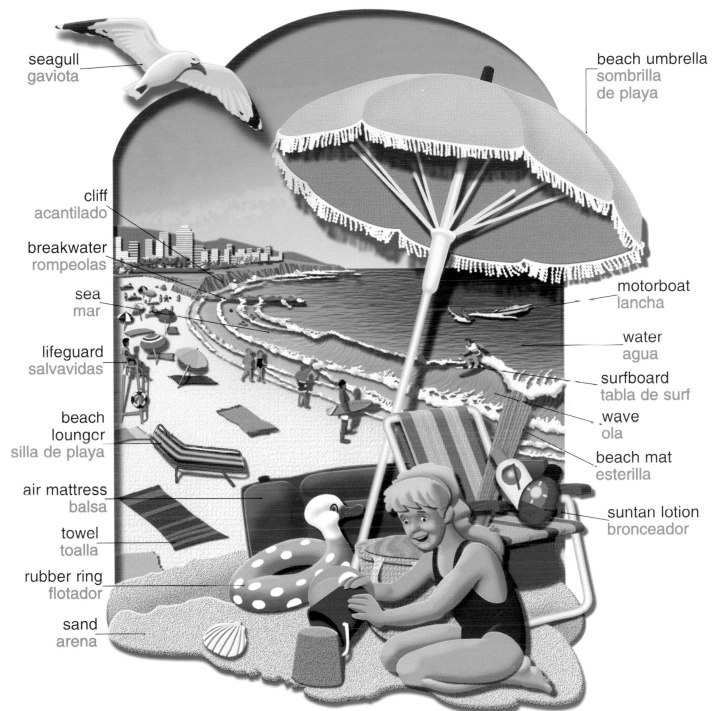

seagull
gaviota

beach umbrella
sombrilla
de playa

cliff
acantilado

breakwater
rompeolas

sea
mar

lifeguard
salvavidas

beach
lounger
silla de playa

air mattress
balsa

towel
toalla

rubber ring
flotador

sand
arena

motorboat
lancha

water
agua

surfboard
tabla de surf

wave
ola

beach mat
esterilla

suntan lotion
bronceador

| to row | to swim | to put on suntan lotion | to sunbathe |
| remar | bañarse | untarse bronceador | broncearse |

Weather/Clima

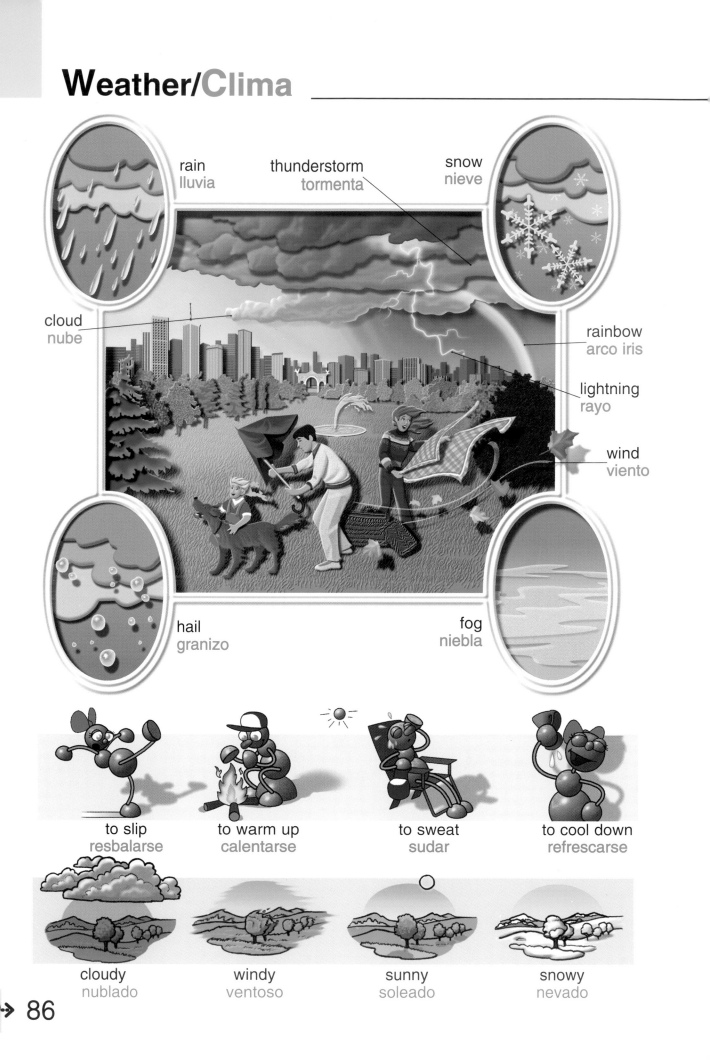

rain
lluvia

thunderstorm
tormenta

snow
nieve

cloud
nube

rainbow
arco iris

lightning
rayo

wind
viento

hail
granizo

fog
niebla

to slip
resbalarse

to warm up
calentarse

to sweat
sudar

to cool down
refrescarse

cloudy
nublado

windy
ventoso

sunny
soleado

snowy
nevado

winter
invierno

spring
primavera

autumn
otoño

summer
verano

to sprout
brotar

to flower
florecer

to sweep
barrer

to plie up
amontonar

autumnal
día otoñal

wintry
día invernal

springlike
día primaveral

summery
día veraniego

87

GLOSSARY/GLOSARIO

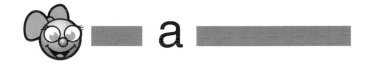 **a**

above: encima, arriba (página 20)
actor: actor (página 66)
actress: actriz (página 66)
to add: sumar (página 26)
address: dirección (página 80)
air conditioning: acondicionador de aire (página 15)
air mattress: (de playa) colchoneta, balsa (página 85)
airplane: avión (página 59)
airport: aeropuerto (página 58)
aisle: pasillo (páginas 59 y 66)
alarm: alarma (página 79)
alarm clock: despertador (página 16)
almond: almendra (página 44)
ambulance: ambulancia (página 78)
amplifier: amplificador (página 69)
anchor: ancla (página 61)
anesthesiologist: anestesista (página 78)
anesthetic: anestesia (página 78)
to anesthetize: anestesiar (página 78)
animal: animal (páginas 28, 40 y 41)
ankle: tobillo (página 6)
to announce: presentar (página 67)
announcer: presentador, -a (página 67)

antenna: antena (páginas 37, 38 y 54)
apartment: apartamento (página 48)
to applaud: aplaudir (página 66)
apple: manzana (página 44)
apple tree: manzano (página 42)
to approach: acercarse (páginas 20 y 83)
apricot: albaricoque, chabacano (página 44)
archaeopteryx: arqueópterix (página 29)
arm: brazo (página 6)
arm chair: butaca (página 15)
arrivals: llegadas (página 56)
artichoke: alcachofa (página 45)
to ask for: pedir (página 48)
asparagus: espárrago (página 45)
asteroid: asteroide (página 83)
athletic shoe: zapato deportivo (páginas 12, 70 y 71)
athletics: atletismo (página 75)
to attack: atacar (página 35)
audience: (en un cine, un teatro) público (página 66)
aunt: tía (página 10)
autumn: otoño (página 87)
autumnal: otoñal (página 87)

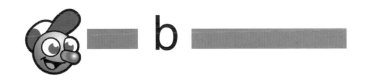 **b**

back: (parte del cuerpo humano) espalda (página 6): (parte del cuerpo de un animal) lomo (páginas 30 y 31)
backboard: (en baloncesto) tablero (página 70)
backstroke: (estilo de natación) espalda (página 73)
baggage truck: camión de equipaje (página 58)
baggy: (de una prenda) flojo, -a (página 13)
balcony: (en un cine, un teatro) balcón (página 66)

91

ball: balón, pelota (páginas 70 y 72)

balloon: (para adornar, para jugar) globo, bomba (página 11)

ballpoint pen: bolígrafo (página 23)

banana: plátano, guineo (página 44)

to bandage: vendar (página 52)

bank: (institución financiera) banco (página 48)

barber: barbero (página 53)

to bark: ladrar (página 30)

barn: (para animales) establo (página 84)

basket: cesta (página 81)

basketball: baloncesto, balón (página 70)

bass: contrabajo (página 68)

bath mat: alfombrilla, alfombra de baño (página 17)

to bathe: bañarse (página 85)

bathroom: cuarto de baño (página 17)

bathtub: bañadera, bañera, tina (página 17)

battery: (de un coche) batería (página 54); (para radios, cámaras...) pila (página 65)

beach: playa (página 85)

beach lounger: silla de playa, tumbona (página 85)

beach mat: esterilla (página 85)

beach umbrella: sombrilla de playa (página 85)

beak: (de un ave) pico (página 33)

bear: oso (página 41)

bed: cama (página 16)

bedroom: dormitorio (página 16)

bedside table: mesita de noche (página 16)

bedspread: sobrecama, colcha (página 16)

bee: abeja (página 38)

beehive: colmena (página 38)

beet: remolacha (página 45)

behind: detrás (página 21)

bell: timbre (página 14 y 55)

below: abajo (página 20)

belt: cinturón, cinto (página 12)

bench: (asiento) banco, banquillo (página 70 y 71)

to bend: doblar (página 71)

beret: boina (página 12)

between: entre (página 21)

bicycle: bicicleta (página 55)

bidet: bidé (página 17)

big: grande (páginas 35 y 55)

birthday cake: bizcocho, tarta, pastel de cumpleaños (página 11)

black: negro (páginas 21 y 25)

blackboard: encerado, pizarra, pizarrón (página 22)

blanket: cobija, manta, friza, frazada (página 16)

to bleat: balar (página 32)

blender: licuadora, batidora (página 18)

blind: persiana (página 16)

to blow: soplar (página 69)

to blow the whistle: tocar el pito, pitar (página 71)

blue: azul (página 25)

board game: tablero, juego de mesa (página 63)

boat: bote, barca, barco (página 60)

body: cuerpo (página 6 y 36)

to boil: hervir (página 45)

bones: huesos (página 7)

book: libro (página 23)

bookshelf: librero (página 15)

bored: aburrido, -a (página 71)

bowl: bol, tazón (página 18)

box: palco (página 66)

brachiosaurus: braquiosaurio (página 28)

brake: freno (página 55)

to brake: frenar (página 54)

branch: rama (página 42)

bread: pan, panadería (página 81)

bread basket: panera (página 19)

breakwater: espigón, rompeolas (página 85)

breaststroke: braza, pecho (página 73)

to breath: respirar (página 73)

bricklayer: albañil (página 52)

bridge: puente (página 50)

brother: hermano (página 10)

brown: marrón, pardo, café (páginas 21 y 24)

to brush your teeth: cepillarse los dientes (página 17)

to build: construir (página 38 y 63)

bulging eyes: ojos saltones (página 36)

bulletin board: tablón de anuncios (página 22)

bumper: parachoques, defensa (página 54)

buoy: boya (página 60)

bus: autobús, omnibus, guagua (página 58)

butcher: carnicero, -a (página 52)

butterfly: (insecto) mariposa (página 37)

butterfly stroke: (estilo de natación) mariposa (página 73)

to button up: abrocharse (página 12)

to buy: compar (página 48)

cab: (en un tren) cabina (página 57)

cabbage: col, repollo (página 45)

cabin: (en un barco) camarote (página 51)

cactus: cactus (página 42)

café: cafetería (página 48)

calculator: calculadora (página 23)

calf: (parte del cuerpo humano) pantorrilla (página 6); (animal) ternero (página 32)

camel: camello (página 31)

camera: cámara (página 65 y 67)

to camp: acampar (página 84)

can opener: abrelatas (página 18)

candle: vela (página 11)

candy: caramelo, dulce (página 11)

cap: gorra (página 12)

car: coche, carro (página 54)

car racetrack: pista de coches (página 63)

car wash: lavadero de carros (página 54)

cards: (para jugar) cartas (página 63)

cargo: carga (página 60)

cargo hold: bodega (página 61)

carnation: clavel (página 43)

carnivorous: canívoro, -a (página 29)

carrot: zanahoria (página 45)

cash register: (en una tienda) caja (página 81)

cashier: cajero, -a (página 81)

castanets: castañuelas (página 69)

castle: castillo (página 63)

cat: gato (página 30)

to catch: atrapar (página 39)

to catch a train: coger un tren (página 56)

caterpillar: gusano, oruga (página 37)

cauliflower: colifor (página 45)

ceiling: techo (página 16)

celery: apio (página 45)

cello: violonchelo (página 68)

cereals: cereales (página 45)

chain: cadena (página 55)

chair: (general) silla (páginas 15 y 77)

chair lift: telesilla (página 74)

chalk: tiza (página 22)

to change channels: seleccionar, cambiar de canal (página 65)

to chase: perseguir (página 34)

check-in: facturación de equipaje (página 58)

cheek: mejilla, cachete (página 6)

cheese: queso (página 81)

cherry: cereza (página 44)

chest: pecho (página 6)

chick: pollito (página 33)

chimney: (de un casa) chimenea (página 14)

chin: barbilla, mentón (página 6)

chocolate: bombón (página 11)

to chop: (cebollas, nueces...) picar (página 18)

chrysalis: crisálida (página 37)

chrysanthemum: crisantemo (página 43)

church: iglesia (página 84)

circle: (figura) círculo (página 27)

city: ciudad (página 48)

clam: almeja (página 40)

clarinet: clarinete (página 69)

classroom: aula (página 22)

claw: uña (página 33 y 34)

clean: limpio, -a (página 13)

cleaning products: artículos de limpieza (página 81)

cliff: acantilado (página 85)

to climb: trepar (página 62)

clippers: tijeras podadoras (página 47)

clock: reloj (página 22 y 56)

close together: juntos, -as (página 14)

closed: cerrado, -a (página 22)

closet: (para ropa) armario, clóset (página 16)

clothes: ropa (página 12)

cloud: nube (página 86)

cloudy: nublado, -a (página 86)

coach: entrenador, -a (página 71)

cockpit: cabina (página 59)

coffee: café (página 81)

coffeemaker: cafetera (página 18)

coffee table: mesa (página 15)

cold: (temperatura) frío (página 9); (enfermedad) catarro (página 76)

cold cuts: fiambres, embutidos (página 81)

colorful: vistoso, -a (página 37)

colors: colores (página 24)

comb: (para el pelo) peine (página 17); (de gallina) cresta (página 33)

to comb your hair: peinarse (página 17)

to come out: salir (página 66)

comet: (en el espacio) cometa (página 83)

comfortable: (confortable) cómodo, -a (página 15)

comforter: edredón, colcha (página 16)

compass: (para dibujar) compás, brújula (página 23)

compsognathus: compsognathus (página 29)

computer: computadora, ordenador (página 16)

conductor: conductor, -a (página 57)

cone: cono (página 27)

constellation: constelación (página 82)

control tower: torre de control (página 58)

cookies: galletas (página 81)

to cool down: refrescarse (página 86)

copilot: copiloto (página 59)

corkscrew: sacacorchos (página 18)

corn: maíz (página 45)

corner: esquina (página 49)

cotton balls: (en hospital) algodón (página 78)

to cough: toser (página 76)

counter: ficha (página 63)

country: (zona rural) campo (página 84)

court: cancha (página 72)

cousin: primo, -a (página 10)

cow: vaca (página 32)

crab: cangrejo, juey (página 40)

crane: grúa (página 60)

crash: accidente (página 51)

to crash: chocar (página 51)

credit card: tarjeta de crédito (página 81)

to croak: croar (página 36)

crocodile: cocodrilo (página 40)

to cross: cruzar (página 49)

crosswalk: paso señalado, paso de peatones (página 49)

to crouch: agacharse (página 6)

to crow: cacarear (página 33)

to cry: llorar (página 10 y 66)

cube: (figura geométrica) cubo (página 27)

cucumber: pepino, pepinillo (página 45)

cup: taza (página 19)

cupboard: (de cocina) armario (página 19)

curious: curioso, -a (página 30)

to curl up: enroscarse (página 34)

curve: curva (página 51)

curtain: telón (página 66)

custard apple: chirimoya (página 44)

customer: comprador, -a (página 81)

customs: aduana (páginas 58 y 60)

cut: cortado, -a (página 11)

to cut: cortar (páginas 18 y 53)

to cut out: (con tijeras) recortar (página 22)

cymbal: (instrumento) platillo (página 69)

 **d**

dahlia: dalia (página 43)

daisy: margarita (página 43)

to dance: bailar (página 68)

dangerous: peligroso, -a (página 49)

dark: (de piel, pelo) trigueño, -a moreno, -a, (de color) oscuro, -a (página 25)

date: dátil (página 44)

decayed tooth: muela cariada (página 77)

to decorate: adornar (página 11)

deflated: desinflado, -a (página 55)

to deliver: entregar (página 80)

dental assistant: ayudante de dentista (página 77)

dentist: dentista (página 77)

departures: salidas (página 56)

desk: pupitre (página 22)

dice: dados (página 63)

dictionary: diccionario (página 23)

to die: morir (página 28)

different: diferente (página 11)

to dig: cavar (página 47)

dinning car: vagón restaurante (página 57)

dinosaurs: dinosaurios (página 28)

diplodocus: diplodoco (página 28)

to direct: dirigir (página 67)

director: directo, -a (página 67)

dirty: sucio, -a (página 13)

to disembark: desembarcar (página 61)

dishwasher: lavaplatos (página 19)

disposable cup: vaso desechable (página 77)

to dive: zambullirse (página 36 y 73)

to dive underwater: sumergirse (página 39)

to divide: dividir (página 26)

diving board: (en natación) trampolín (página 73)

to dock: (en un puerto) atracar (página 60)

doctor: médico, -a doctor, a- (página 76)

dog: perro (página 30)

dog house: perrera, caseta de perro (página 14)

doll: (juguete) muñeco, -a (página 63)

dollhouse: casa de muñecas (página 63)

dolly: carrito (página 56)

dolphin: delfín (página 40)

dominoes: dominó (página 63)

door: puerta (página 14)

doorbell: (de la puerta) timbre (página 14)

downhill ski trail: pista de esquí (página 74)

drain: alcantarilla (página 49)

to draw: dibujar (página 24)

to dribble: driblar (página 70)

drill: torno, taladro (página 77)

to drink: libar (página 38)

drinks: bebidas (página 81)

to drive: manejar, conducir (página 54)

drone: zángano (página 38)

drum: tambor (página 69)

drum set: (instrumento) batería (página 69)

to dry yourself: secarse (página 17)

 **e**

eagle: águila (página 41)

ear: oreja (páginas 8 y 30)

earth: tierra (página 46)

Earth: Tierra (páginas 82 y 83)

edge: borde (página 73)

egg: huevo (páginas 33 y 37)

eggplant: berenjena (página 45)

eight: ocho (página 26)

eighteen: dieciocho (página 26)

eighth: octavo, -a (página 27)

eighty: ochenta (página 26)

elbow: codo (página 6)

electric guitar: guitarra eléctrica (página 69)

electric keyboard: órgano electrónico (páginas 65 y 68)

electrician: electricista (página 52)

elephant: elefante (página 41)

eleven: once (página 26)

elm: olmo (página 42)

to embark: embarcar (página 61)

emergency room: sala de emergencias, sala de urgencias (página 78)

empty: vacío, -a (página 38)

encyclopedia: enciclopedia (página 22)

engine: (de un coche) motor (página 54); (de un tren) máquina, locomotora (página 57)

engine room: sala de máquinas (página 61)

engineer: (de un tren) maquinista (página 61)

envelope: (para cartas) sobre (página 80)

to erase: borrar (página 22); goma de borrar (página 23)

eraser: borrador (página 22)

to escape: escapar (página 34)

to examine: examinar (página 76)

excited: animado, -a (página 71)

exhaust pipe: tubo de escape: (página 55)

to explain: explicar, informar (página 58)

eye: ojo (páginas 9, 30, 35, 37 y 39)

eyebrow: ceja (página 9)

eyelashes: pestañas (página 9)

eyelid: párpado (páginas 9 y 34)

 **f**

to face: enfrentarse (página 20)

fair: (apariencia física) rubio, -a (página 6)

family: familia (página 10)

far: lejos (página 20)

far apart: separados, -as (página 14)

farmer: agricultor, -a (página 53)

fast: rápido (página 54)

to fasten your seat belt: abrocharse el cinturón de seguridad (página 59)

fat: gordo, -a (página 6)

father: padre (página 10)

faucet: grifo, pila, llave (página 17)

fax: fax (página 80)

feather: (de ave) pluma (página 33)

to feel dizzy: marearse (página 79)

fence: valla, cerca (páginas 14 y 46)

field: campo, cultivo (página 84)

fierce: gruñón, -a (página 30)

fifteen: quince (página 26)

fifth: quinto, -a (página 26)

fifty: cincuenta (página 26)

fig: higo (página 44)

filled tooth: muela empastada (página 77)

film: película (página 66)

to film: filmar (página 64)

fin: (de un pez) aleta (página 25)

fine: fino, -a (página 25)

finger: dedo (página 6)

fir: abeto (página 42)

fire engine: bomba de incendios, coche de bomberos (página 79)

firefighter: bombero -a (página 79)

fire station: estación de bomberos (página 79)

first: primero, -a (página 26)

fish: pescado, pescadería (página 81)

fish dealer: pescadero, -a (página 52)

fisherman: pescador, -a (página 53)

fishing boat: pesquero (página 60)

five: cinco (página 26)

flamingo: (ave) flamenco (página 40)

flash: flash (página 65)

flight attendant: azafata, auxiliar de vuelo (página 59)

flipper: (para nadar) aleta (página 73)

to float: flotar (páginas 61 y 73)

flock: (de ovejas) rebaño (páginas 32 y 84)

floor: (de una habitación) suelo (página 16)

flower: flor (páginas 43 y 46)

to flower: florecer (página 87)

flower bed: jardín de flores, parterre (página 46)

flute: flauta (página 69)

to fly: volar (páginas 28 y 59)

to fly away: alejarse volando (página 83)

foal: (caballo joven) potro (página 31)

fog: niebla (página 86)

foot: pie (página 23)

footbridge: puente de peatones, paso elevado (página 50)

forehead: (parte del cuerpo humano) frente (página 6)

fork: (para comer) tenedor (página 18); (para cavar) escarbador, horquilla (página 47)

forty: cuarenta (página 26)

fountain pen: pluma fuente (página 23)

four: cuatro (página 26)

fourteen: catorce (página 26)

fourth: cuarto, -a (página 26)

freestyle: (en natación) libre (página 73)

freight train: tren de carga (página 57)

freighter: carguero (página 60)

friendly: cariñoso, -a (página 30)

frightened: asustado, -a (página 30)

frog: rana (página 36)

front leg: pata delantera (página 30)

frozen food: congelados (página 81)

fruit: fruta, frutos (páginas 44 y 81)

to fry: freír (página 19)

fuel: combustible (página 58)

full: lleno, -a (página 38)

funnel: (de un barco) chimenea (página 61)

fur: pelo, lana (página 30)

galaxy: galaxia (página 82)

to gallop: galopar (página 31)

game: juego (página 621 y 63)

garage: garaje (página 14)

garden: jardín (páginas 46 y 47)

gardener: jardinero, -a (página 46)

garland: guirnalda (página 11)

garlic: ajo (página 45)

gas station: gasolinera (página 51)

to get dressed: vestirse (página 12)

to get undressed: desvestirse (página 12)

to get up: levantarse (página 16)

gift: regalo (página 11)

gigantic: gigantesco, -a (página 29)

gill: agalla (página 35)

giraffe: jirafa (página 41)

to give a gift: regalar (página 11)

glass: vaso (página 18)

globe: globo terráqueo (página 22)

glove: guante (página 74)

to go away: alejarse (página 20)

to go down: bajar (páginas 14); lanzarse (página 62); descender (página 74)

to go in: entrar (página 66)

to go through: pasar (página 75)

to go up: subir (página 14); ascender (página 74)

goal: (en fútbol) portería (página 71)

goalkeeper: (en fútbol) portero (página 71)

goalpost: larguero, poste (página 71)

goggles: gafas protectores (página 73); gafas (página 74)

gorilla: gorila (página 41)

to graft: injertar (página 42)

grandfather: abuelo (página 10)

grandmother: abuela (página 10)

grape: uva (página 44)

grapefruit: toronja, pomelo (página 44)

grass: hierba (página 46)

to grate: rallar (página 18)

grater: guayo, rallador (página 18)

gray: gris (páginas 21 y 24)

green: verde (página 24)

green bean: habichuela, ejote (página 45)

greenhouse: invernadero (página 46)

grocer: frutero, -a (página 52)

grocery bag: bolsa de compras (página 81)

to grow: crecer (página 42)

gymnastics: gimnasia (página 75)

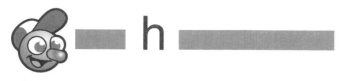

h

hail: granizo (página 86)

hairdresser: peluquero, -a (página 53)

hairdryer: secador de pelo (página 17)

hand: mano (página 6)

handlebars: manubrio, manillar (página 55)

hangar: hangar (página 58)

hanger: gancho, percha, perchero
(página 16)

happy: contento, -a (página 10)

hard: duro, -a (página 9)

hardworking: trabajador, -a (página 38)

harp: arpa (página 68)

to hatch: nacer (página 28)

hazelnut: avellana (página 44)

head: cabeza (páginas 6, 36, 37 y 39)

headache: dolor de cabeza (página 76)

headlight: (de un coche) faro, farol
(página 54)

headphones: auriculares (página 64)

health: salud (página 76)

to hear: oír (página 8)

hearing: oído (página 8)

heavy: pesado (página 29)

hedge: seto (página 46)

helmet: (para la cabeza) casco
(páginas 55 y 79)

hen: gallina (página 33)

herbivorous: herbívoro, -a (página 29)

hide: (de un animal) piel (página 32)

to hide: ocultarse (página 39)

hide-and-seek: (juego) escondite (página 62)

high jump: salto de altura (página 75)

highway: autopista (página 50)

hill: colina, loma, monte (página 84)

hind leg: pata trasera (página 30)

hip: cadera (página 6)

hippopotamus: hipopótamo (página 40)

to hit: golpear (página 72)

honey: miel (página 38)

honeycomb: panal (página 38)

hood: capó (página 54)

hoof: casco, pezuña (páginas 31 y 32)

hoop: aro (páginas 70 y 75)

horn: cuerno (página 32)

horse: caballo (página 31); (de gimansia)
potro (página 75)

hose: manguera (páginas 47 y 79)

hospital: hospital (página 78)

hot: caliente (página 9)

hotel: hotel (página 48)

house: casa (página 14)

to hug: abrazar (página 11)

hump: joroba (página 31)

hungry: hambriento, -a (página 37)

hyacinth: jacinto (página 43)

hydrangea: hortensia (página 43)

hyena: hiena (página 41)

i

in: dentro, en (página 21)

in front of: delante (páginas 20 y 21)

information board: panel de información
(página 56)

to inspect: inspeccionar (página 58)

instruments: instrumentos
(páginas 68, 77 y 78)

iris: iris (página 9)

ironed: planchado, -a (página 12)

j

jacket: chaqueta (impermeable), cazadora,
anorak (páginas 12 y 74)

jaw: mandíbula, quijada (página 35)
jet engine: motor de propulsión (página 59)
jetty: embarcadero (página 60)
jigsaw puzzle: rompecabezas (página 63)
job: trabajo (páginas 52 y 53)
joints: articulaciones (página 7)
juice: zumo, jugo (página 11)
juicer: exprimidora (página 18)
to jump: saltar, brincar (página 6, 36, 74 y 75)

kangaroo: canguro (página 41)
kettle drum: (instrumento) timbal (página 68)
to kick: patear, dar un puntapié (página 71)
to kiss: besar (página 11)
kitchen: cocina (página 18)
kite: (para jugar) papalote, cometa (página 62)
kiwi: (fruta) kiwi (página 44)
knee: rodilla (página 61)
knee pad: rodillera (página 70)
knife: cuchillo (página 18)

ladder: escalera (página 79)
ladle: cucharón (página 19)
lamb: cordero (página 32)
lamp: lámpara (páginas 15 y 77)
to land: aterrizar (página 59); alunizar (página 83)
land animal: animal terrestre (página 34)
lane: (en una carretera) carril (página 50)
to laugh: reír (páginas 10 y 66)
lawn mower: cortacésped, podadora (página 47)

lawyer: abogado, -a (página 52)
leaf: (de una planta) hoja (página 42)
to lean out: asomarse (página 14)
leek: ajo porro, puerro (página 45)
leg: (de una persona) pierna (página 6); (de un animal) pata (páginas 34 y 36)
legumes: legumbres (página 45)
leisure activities: entretenimientos (página 62)
lemon: limón (página 44)
lentil: lenteja (página 45)
leopard: leopardo (página 41)
letter: (para enviar) carta (página 80)
letter carrier: cartero (página 80)
lettuce: lechuga (página 45)
library: biblioteca (página 48)
to lick: lamer (página 30)
to lie down: acostarse (páginas 6 y 15)
lifeboat: bote salvavidas (página 61)
lifeguard: salvavidas, socorrista (página 85)
light: (de color) claro, -a (página 25); (de peso) ligero, -a (páginas 29 y 37); (en un estudio de televisión) foco (página 67)
lighthouse: (para barcos) faro (página 67)
lightning: rayo, relámpago (pagina 86)
lily: lirio (página 43)
lima bean: haba lima (pagina 45)
line judge: (en tenis) juez de línea (página 72)
linesman: (en fútbol) juez de línea (página 71)
lion: león (página 41)
lip: labio (páginas 9 y 31)
to listen: escuchar (página 64)
living room: (en una casa) sala, salón (página 15)
to load: cargar (página 56)
lock: (cerradura) seguro (página 54)
locker: consigna automática (página 56)
long: largo, -a (página 12)
to look: mirar (página 49)
to look out: vigilar (página 35)
to love: querer (página 10)
luggage: equipaje (página 57)
luggage rack: portaequipaje (página 57)

m

mailbox: buzón (páginas 49 y 80)

mane: crin, melena (página 31)

map: mapa (página 22)

maraca: maraca (página 69)

marbles: canicas, bolitas (página 62)

marine animal: animal marino
(página 34)

mat: (de gimnasia) colchoneta (página 75)

meat: carne (página 81)

mechanic: mecánico (página 51)

medium-sized: mediano, -a (página 55)

melon: melón (página 44)

to meow: maullar (página 30)

messy: desordenado, -a (página 15)

microphone: micrófono (página 67)

microwave oven: microondas (página 19)

milk: leche (página 81)

to milk: ordeñar (página 32)

mirror: espejo (página 17); espejo retrovisor
(página 55)

to miss a train: perder un tren (página 56)

model: (moda, de fotografía) modelo
(página 53)

modeling clay: plastilina, masilla (página 23)

modern: moderno, -a (página 54)

money: dinero (página 81)

money order: giro postal (página 80)

monitor: (pantalla) monitor (página 67)

to moo: mugir (página 32)

moon: Luna (página 83)

mother: madre (página 10)

motor: (de una moto) motor (página 55)

motorboat: lancha (página 85

motorcycle: moto (página 55)

mountain: montaña (página 84)

mouth: boca (página 35)

movie theater: cine (páginas 48 y 66)

to multiply: multiplicar (página 26)

muscles: músculos (página 7)

muscular: musculoso, -a (página 7)

museum: museo (página 48)

mushroom: champiñón (página 45)

stereo system: equipo de sonido (página 16)

musical instruments: instrumentos musicales
(página 68)

n

name: nombre (página 80)

napkin: servilleta (página 19)

near: cerca (página 20)

nebula: nebulosa (página 82)

neck: cuello (páginas 6 y 31)

to neigh: relinchar (página 31)

nervous: nervioso, -a (página 71)

net: (en fútbol, tenis) red (páginas 71 y 72)

new: nuevo, -a (página 14)

newsstand: quiosco (página 49)

nightgown: camisón (página 13)

nine: nueve (página 26)

nineteen: diecinueve (página 26)

ninety: noventa (página 26)

ninth: noveno, -a (página 27)

noisy: ruidoso, -a (páginas 10 y 48)

nose: nariz (página 8); (de un animal) hocico
(página 30)

nostril: fosa nasal (página 8)

notebook: cuaderno (página 23)

notepad: bloc (página 23)

number: número (página 26)

nurse: enfermero, -a (página 77)

to nurse: cuidar a un enfermo (página 76)

nut: fruto seco (página 44)

o

oak: roble (página 42)
obedient: obediente (página 32)
octopus: pulpo (página 39)
to oil: (con aceite) engrasar (página 55)
oil tanker: (barco) petrolero (página 60)
ointment: pomada (página 76)
old: viejo, -a (páginas 10 y 14)
olive tree: olivo (página 42)
on: encima (página 20)
on the left: a la izquierda (página 21)
on the right: a la derecha (página 21)
one: uno (página 26)
one hundred: cien (página 26)
one million: un millón (página 26)one thousand: mil (página 26)
onion: cebolla (página 45)
open: abierto, -a (página 22)
to operate: operar (página 78)
operating room: quirófano, sala de operaciones (página 78)
orange: (color) anaranjado, -a (página 24); (fruta) naranja, china (página 44)
orchestra: orquesta (página 66)
ostrich: avestruz (página 41)
out: fuera (página 21)
outside: por fuera (página 14)
to overtake: adelantar (página 20)

p

package: paquete (página 80)
to paint: pintar (página 24)
painter: pintor, -a (página 53)
pajamas: pijama (página 13)
palm: (árbol) palmera (página 42)

pansy: (flor) pensamiento (página 43)
panties: pantaloncitos, bragas, pantaletas (página 13)
pants: pantalón (página 12)
paper clip: presilla, sujeta papeles (página 23)
parallel bars: (en gimnasia) paralelas (página 75)
parasauolophus: parasaurolophus (página 28)
to park: aparcar, estacionar (página 50)
parrot: papagayo (página 41)
parsley: perejil (página 45)
party: fiesta (página 11)
party hat: gorro de papel (página 11)
to pass: (un carro) pasar (página 50); (una pelota) pasar (página 70)
passenger: pasajero, -a (páginas 57 y 59)
passenger train: tren de pasajeros (página 57)
passport: pasaporte (página 58)
pastries: pastelitos (página 11)
path: camino, sendoro (página 46)
patient: (persona enferma) paciente (páginas 76 y 78)
paw: garra (página 30)
pea: guisante, chícharo (página 45)
peach: durazno, melocotón (página 44)
peanut: cacahuate, cacahuete, maní (página 44)
pear: pera (página 44)
to peck: picotear (página 33)
pedal: pedal (página 55)
to pedal: pedalear (página 55)
pedestrian zone: calle peatonal, zona peatonal (página 48)
to peel: pelar (página 19)
pen: corral (páginas 32 y 84)
pencil: lápiz (página 23)
pencil case: estuche de lápices (página 23)
pencil sharpener: sacapuntas (página 23)
penguin: pingüino (página 40)

personal radio cassette player: radiocasete personal (página 64)

petal: pétalo (página 43)

petunia: petunia (página 43)

pharmacist: (persona) farmacéutico, -a (página 23)

pharmacy: farmacia (página 48)

photocopier: fotocopiadora (página 22)

photographer: fotógrafo, -a (página 53)

piano: piano (página 68)

picture: (pintura) cuadro (página 15)

pier: (en un puerto) muelle (página 60)

pigsty: pocilga (página 84)

to pile up: amontononar (página 87)

pills: píldoras, pastillas (página 76)

pillow: almohada (página 16)

pilot: (de un avión) piloto (página 59)

pine: pino (página 42)

pine nut: piñón (página 44)

pineapple: piña (página 44)

pink: (color) rosado -a, rosa (página 24)

pistachio: pistacho (página 44)

pitcher: jarra (página 19)

planet: planeta (página 83)

plant: planta (página 83)

to plant: plantar (página 47)

plate: plato (página 18)

platform: andén (página 56)

to play: (un juego) jugar (página 63); (un instrumento) tocar (página 65)

player: jugador, -a (páginas 70, 71 y 72)

playful: juguetón, a- (página 32)

playing field: campo de fútbol (página 71)

to plough: arar (página 84)

to plug in: enchufar (página 65)

plum: ciruela (página 44)

plumber: plomero, fontanero, -a (página 52)

poisonous: venenoso, -a (página 34)

pole: (para esquiar) bastón (página 74)

pole vault: salto con garrocha, salto con pértiga (página 75)

police officer: policía (página 50)

polite: amable (página 49)

poplar: álamo (página 42)

port: (para barcos) puerto (página 60)

porter: (personas) maletero, mozo de estación (página 56)

porthole: (en un barco) ojo de buey, claraboya (página 61)

post office: oficina de correos (página 80)

postal code: código postal (página 80)

postcard: tarjeta postal (página 80)

poster: cartel, póster (página 16)

potato: papa, patata (página 45)

prescription: (del médico) receta (página 76)

pretty: bonito, -a (página 43)

projector: proyector (página 22)

propeller: hélice (página 61)

prow: proa (página 61)

to pump up: (un neumático) inflar (página 55)

to puncture: poncharse, pinchar (página 54)

pupil: pupila (página 9); alumno, -a (página 22)

puppet theater: guiñol (página 63)

purple: violeta, morado (página 25)

to push: empujar (páginas 15, 54 y 70)

to put on: ponerse (página 13)

to put on makeup: maquillar (página 67)

to put on suntan lotion: untarse bronceador (página 85)

to put out: apagar (página 79)

queen bee: abeja reina (página 38)

quiet: tranquilo, -a, silencio, -a (páginas 10 y 48)

quiet street: calle silenciosa (página 48)

r

radar: radar (páginas 58 y 61)

radiator: radiador (página 15)

radio: radio (página 65)

radio cassette player: radiocasetera (página 16)

radish: rábano (página 45)

rain: lluvia (página 86)

rainbow: arco iris (páginas 24 y 86)

rake: rastrillo (página 47)

raquet: raqueta (página 72)

raspberry: frambuesas (página 44)

reading lamp: lámpara,flexo (página 16)

record: (de música) disco (página 16)

to record: (sonidos) grabar (página 64)

record player: tocadiscos (página 22)

rectangle: rectángulo (página 27)

rectangular: rectangular (página 27)

red: rojo (página 25)

red pepper: pimiento rojo (página 45)

referee: (en fútbol, baloncesto) árbitro (páginas 70 y 71)

refrigerator: refrigerador, frigorífico, refrigeradora, nevera (página 18)

remote control: control remoto, mando a distancia (página 64)

reporter: periodista (página 53)

to rescue: rescatar (página 79)

to rest: descansar (página 52)

rest area: área de descanso (página 50)

restroom: baño, retrete (página 56)

to return: (en tenis) devolver (página 72)

ribs: (huesos) costillas (página 7)

rice: arroz (página 45)

to ring: (una campana, un timbre) tocar (página 15)

ripe: (fruta, verdura) maduro, -a (página 44)

to rise: (el sol) salir (página 82)

river: río (página 84)

road: avenida, carretera (página 49)

road sign: señal de tráfico (página 49)

robe: bata (página 13)

robot: robot (página 63)

roller skates: patines de ruedas (página 62)

roof: tejado, techo (página 14)

root: raíz (página 42)

rose: (flor) rosa (página 43)

rotten: podrido, -a (página 44)

round: redondo, -a (página 27)

to row: remar (página 85)

rubber ring: (en la cintura) flotador (página 85)

rudder: timón (página 61)

rude: descortés, maleducado, -a, (página 49)

rug: alfombra (página 15)

ruler: (para trazar líneas) regla (página 23)

to run: correr (páginas 6, 30 y 75)

runner: corredor, -a (página 75)

running track: pista para carreras (página 75)

runway: pista de aterrizaje (página 58)

s

sad: triste (página 10)

safe: (protegido) seguro, -a (página 49)

to sail: navegar (página 60)

sailboat: velero (página 60)

same: igual (página 11)

sand: arena (página 85)

sardine: sardina (página 53)

satellite: satélite artificial (página 83)

satellite dish: antena de satélite, antena parabólica (página 14)

to save: (fútbol) parar un gol (página 71)

saxophone: saxofón (página 69)

scales: escamas (página 34 y 35)

to scare: espantar (página 84)

scarecrow: espantapájaros (página 84)

scenery: decorado (página 66)

school: colegio (página 22)

school bag: (para el colegio) mochila, bulto (página 23)

to score: encestar, colar la pelota (página 70)

scoreboard: marcador (página 71)

to scratch: arañar (página 30); escarbar (página 33)

screen: pantalla (página 66)

to scribble: pintarrajear, garabatear (página 24)

sea: mar (página 85)

seagull: gaviota (páginas 40 y 85)

seal: foca (página 40)

seasons: (del año) estaciones (página 87)

seat: asiento (páginas 54, 55 y 57)

seat belt: cinturón de seguridad (página 54)

second: segundo, -a (página 26)

to see: ver (página 8)

seed: semilla (página 46)

seesaw: (para jugar) balancín, cachumbambé, subibaja (página 62)

senses: (vista, oído...) sentidos (páginas 8 y 9)

to serve: (tenis) sacar, lanzar (página 72)

service station: área de servicios (página 51)

services: servicios (páginas 78 a 81)

serving dish: (plato) fuente (página 19)

to set: (el Sol) ponerse (página 82)

to set sail: zarpar (página 60)

seven: siete (página 26)

seventeen: diecisiete (página 26)

seventh: séptimo, -a (página 27)

seventy: setenta (página 26)

to shake: sacudir (página 69)

shaker: cubilete (página 63)

shampoo: champú (página 17)

shapes: figuras (página 26)

shark: tiburón (página 35)

sharp: afilado, -a (página 35)

to shear: esquilar (página 32)

sheep: oveja (página 32)

sheet: sábana (página 16

shelf: estante (página 81)

shell: caparazón (página 34); concha (página 39)

sheperd: pastor, -a (página 84)

shin guard: espinillera (página 71)

to shine: brillar (página 82)

ship: barco (página 61)

shirt: camisa (página 12); camiseta (página 71)

shoe: zapato (página 12)

shop: (comercio) tienda (página 49)

short: (referido a estatura) bajo, -a (páginas 6 y 70); (referido a longitud) corto, -a (página 12)

shoulder: hombro (página 6)

to shout: gritar (página 10)

shovel: (para cavar) pala (página 47)

to show: (mostrar) enseñar (página 58)

shower: ducha, regadera (página 17)

shower cap: gorro de ducha (página 17)

shower curtain: cortina de ducha, cortina de baño (página 17)

shrimp: camarón (página 40)

sidewalk: acera, banqueta (página 49)

sight: (visión) vista (página 9)

to sign: firmar (página 80)

silo: silo (página 84)

to sing: cantar (página 68)

sink: lavamanos (página 17); lavabo (página 77)

to sink: (barco) hundirse (página 61)

siren: (alarma) sirena (página 78)

sister: hermana (página 10)

to sit: sentarse (página 15)

six: seis (página 26)

sixteen: dieciséis (página 26)

sixth: sexto, -a (página 27)

sixty: sesenta (página 26)

to skate: patinar (página 62)

skateboard: monopatín (página 62)

skeleton: esqueleto (página 7)

ski: esquí (página 74)

to ski: esquiar (página 74)

ski boot: (calzado) bota de esquí (páginas 70, 71 y 74)

ski pants: pantalones de esquí (página 74)

ski resort: estación de esquí (página 74)

skier: esquiador, -a (página 74)

skiing: (deporte) esquí (página 74)

skin: (de una persona, de un animal) piel (páginas 8 y 36)

skinny: huesudo, -a, flaco, -a (página 7)

skipping rope: cuerda de saltar (página 62)

skirt: falda, saya, pollera (página 12)

skull: cráneo (página 7)

skyscraper: rascacielos (página 48)

to sleep: dormir (página 16)

sleeping car: coche cama, vagón de literas (página 57)

to slice: rebanar (página 45)

slide: tobogán, canal, resbaladilla (página 62)

slime: (de caracol) baba (página 39)

to slip: resbalarse (página 86)

slipper: zapatilla, pantufla (página 13)

slippery: resbaladizo, -a (página 35)

to slither: reptar (página 34)

slow: lento, -a (página 34)

small: pequeño, -a (página 35 y 55)

smell: olfato (página 8)

to smell: oler (página 8)

snail: caracol (página 39)

snake: serpiente, culebra, víbora (página 34)

to sneeze: estornudar (página 76)

snow: nieve (página 86)

snowy: nevado, -a (página 86)

soap: jabón (página 17)

soccer: fútbol (página 71)

soccer ball: (para jugar al fútbol) pelota, balón (página 71)

sock: calcetín, media (página 12)

sofa: sofá (página 15)

soft: blando, -a (páginas 9 y 39)

son: hijo (página 10)

sound engineer: técnico de sonido (página 67)

soup bowl: plato hondo (página 18)

to sow: sembrar (página 84)

spaceship: nave espacial (página 82)

sparrow: gorrión (página 33)

spawn: huevo (página 36)

speaker: (de un equipo de música) altavoz, bocina (página 65)

spectators: (en un estadio de fútbol) público (página 71)

sphere: esfera (página 27)

to spin: girar (página 7)

spinach: espinaca (página 45)

spine: columna vertebral (página 7)

spiral: espiral (página 39)

sponge: esponja (página 17)

spoon: cuchara (página 18)

sports: deportes (página 70)

to spray: fumigar (página 42)

spring: manantial (página 84); primavera (página 87)

springlike: primaveral (página 87)

to sprout: (plantas) brotar (página 87)

square: (figura) cuadro (página 27)

squid: calamar (página 40)

stadium: estadio (página 71)

stage: (de teatro) escenario (página 66)

stair truck: (de un avión) furgón de escalerrilla (página 51)

stalk: tallo (página 43)

stamp: (de correos) sello, estampilla, timbre (página 80)

to stamp: (con un sello de goma) sellar (página 80)

stapler: grapadora, engrapadora, presilladora (página 23)

star: estrella (página 82)

starfish: estrella de mar (página 40)

station: (de tren) estación (página 56)

stationmaster: jefe de estación (página 54)

to stay at: hospedarse (página 48)

steering wheel: (de un coche) volante, timón (página 54)

stegosaurus: estegosaurio (página 29)

steps: (en el exterior de una casa) escalera (página 14); (un avión, una piscina) escalerilla (páginas 59 y 73)

stereo system: equipo de sonido (página 16)

stern: popa (página 61)

stethoscope: estetoscopio (página 78)

sticky: pegajoso, -a (página 36)

to sting: (abeja) picar (página 38)

stinger: aguijón (página 38)

to stir: revolver (página 18)

to stop: parar (página 51); detenerse (página 55)

stove: estufa, cocina (página 19)

straw: paja (página 33)

strawberry: fresa (página 44)

street: calle (página 49)

streetlight: farol (página 49)

to stretch: estirarse (página 7)

strong: fuerte (página 7)

to strum: rasguear (página 69)

studio: (de televisión) estudio (página 67)

to study: estudiar (página 22)

substitute: (en deporte) suplente (página 70)

to subtract: (en matemáticas) restar (página 26)

subway: tren, metro subterráneo (página 48)

sucker: (de un pulpo) ventosa (página 39)

sugar bowl: azucarera, azucarero (página 19)

suitcase: maleta (página 56)

summer: verano (página 87)

summery: veraniego, -a (página 87)

sun: Sol (página 82)

to sunbathe: tomar el sol, broncearse (página 85)

sunny: soleado, -a (página 86)

suntan lotion: bronceador (página 85)

supermarket: supermercado (página 81)

surfboard: tabla de surf (página 85)

surgeon: cirujano, -a (página 78)

to swallow: tragar (página 35)

to sweat: sudar (página 86)

sweater: suéter (página 12)

to sweep: barrer (página 87)

sweetsmelling: perfumado, -a (página 43)

to swim: nadar (página 28); bañarse (página 85)

to swim underwater: bucear (página 73)

swimming: natación (página 83)

swimming cap: gorra de nadar (página 73)

swimming pool: piscina, alberca (página 73)

swimming trunks: (de hombre) bañador, trusa (página 73)

swimsuit: (de mujer) traje de baño (página 73)

swing: columpio, balance (página 62)

to swing: columpiarse, mecerse (página 62); balancearse (página 75)

swiss chard: acelga (página 45)

swollen gum: encía hinchada (página 77)

swordfish: pez espada (página 40)

syringe: jeringuilla (página 78)

syrup: jarabe (página 76)

table: mesa (página 18)

tablecloth: mantel (página 19)

tadpole: renacuajo (página 36)

tail: (de un animal, un avión) cola (páginas 30, 33, 34, 35, y 59)

to take off: (una prenda de ropa) quitarse (página 13); (un avión) despegar (página 59)

to take photos: sacar fotos (página 53 y 64)

to take pulse: tomar el pulso (página 78)

to take a shower: ducharse (página 17)

tall: alto, -a (páginas 6 y 7)

tambourine: pandereta (página 69)

tame: manso, -a (página 31)

tangerine: mandarina (página 44)

to tap your feet: zapatear (página 68)

tape: cinta adhesiva, esparadrapo (página 78)

taste: (sentido) gusto (página 9)

to taste: (comida, bebida) probar (página 8)

tawny: (de pelo, pelaje) atrigado, de color rojizo (página 21)

taxi driver: taxista (página 53)

tea: té (página 81)

to teach: (una asignatura) enseñar (página 53)

teacher: profesor, -a, maestro, -a (páginas 22 y 52)

teapot: tetera (página 19)

teddybear: oso de peluche (página 63)

teeth: dientes (páginas 7 y 31)

telephone: teléfono (página 15)

telephone booth: cabina de teléfonos (página 49)

television: televisión (páginas 15 y 64)

television studio: estudio de televisión (página 67)

ten: diez (página 26)

tendons: tendones (página 7)

tennis: tenis (página 72)

tentacle: tentáculo (página 39)

tenth: décimo, -a (página 27)

theater: teatro, cine (páginas 48 y 66)

thermometer: termómetro (página 76)

thick: (objeto) grueso, -a (página 25)

thigh: muslo (página 6)

thin: delgado, -a (página 6)

thirteen: trece (página 26)

thirty: treinta (página 26)

three: tres (página 26)

to throw: (arrojar) lanzar, tirar (página 71)

to throw away: tirar a la basura, botar (página 48)

to throw up: vomitar (página 76)

thunderstorm: tormenta (página 86)

ticket: (de transporte) boleto, billete (páginas 56 y 58)

ticket office: taquilla (página 56)

tidy: ordenado, -a (página 15 y 46)

to tidy up: ordenar (página 63)

tiger: tigre (página 41)

tight: ceñido, -a, apretado, -a (página 13)

tights: leotardos, medias (página 12)

tire: llanta, neumático (página 54)

tired: cansado, -a (página 70)

toaster: tostadora (página 19)

toe: dedo del pie (página 6)

toilet: inodoro (página 17)

toilet paper: papel sanitario (página 17)

toll booth: (lugar) peaje (página 45)

tomato: tomate, jitomate (página 45)

tongue: (de una persona, un animal) lengua (páginas 9, 34 y 36)

tools: herramientas (página 47)

toolshed: (en un jardín) cobertizo (página 46)

tooth: diente (páginas 35 y 77)

toothbrush: cepillo de dientes (página 17)

toothpaste: pasta de dientes (página 17)

tortoise: tortuga (página 34)

touch: (sentido) tacto (página 8)

to touch: (con las manos) tocar (página 8)

to tow: remolcar (página 51)

tow truck: (para vehículos averiados) grúa (página 51)

towel: toalla (páginas 17 y 85)

toy: juguete (página 63)

toy car: coche o carro de juguete v 63)

track: vía, línea (página 57)

tractor: tractor (página 84)

traffic light: semáforo (página 49)

train: tren (páginas 56 y 57)

trainer: masajista (página 71)

transport: transporte (página 54)

trash bin: (para basura) contenedor, basurero, papelera, safacón (páginas 14 y 49)

tray: bandeja (página 19)

tree: árbol (página 42)

triangle: triángulo (página 27)

triangular: triangular (página 27)

triceratops: triceratops (página 28)

tricycle: triciclo (página 62)

trombone: trombón (página 69)

to trot: trotar (página 31)

trowel: (de jardinero) paleta (página 47)

truck: camión (página 50)

trumpet: trompeta (página 69)

trunk: (parte de un árbol) tronco (página 42); (de un coche) maletero, cajuela, baúl (página 54)

T-shirt: camiseta (página 13)

tugboat: remolcador (página 60)

tulip: tulipán (página 43)

tunnel: túnel (página 50)

tureen: sopera (página 19)

to turn: (para cambiar de dirección) girar, doblar (página 50)

to turn into: transformarse (página 36)

to tweet: piar (página 33)

twelve: doce (página 26)

twenty: veinte (página 26)

two: dos (página 26)

tyrannosaurus: tiranosaurio (página 29)

V

vase: florero (página 18)

VCR: vídeo, videocasetera (página 64)

vegetables: verduras, vegetales (páginas 45 y 81)

veterinarian: veterinario, -a (página 52)

video camera: cámara de vídeo (página 65)

videocassette: videocasete (página 64)

video-game: videojuego, videoconsola (páginas 63 y 64)

village: pueblo (página 84)

vintage: (coche) antiguo (página 54)

violet: (flor) violeta (página 43)

violin: violîn (página 68)

U

umpire: (en balonceto, tenis) juez (página 70)

to unbutton: desabrocharse (página 12)

uncle: tío (página 10)

uncomfortable: (silla) incómodo, -a (página 15)

under: debajo (página 20)

underpants: calzoncillo (página 13)

universe: universo (página 82)

to unload: descargar (página 56)

to unplug: desenchufar (página 65)

unripe: (fruta) verde (página 44)

untidy: descuidado, -a (página 46)

usher: acomodador, -a (página 66)

utensils: (de cocina) utensilios (página 19)

W

waist: cintura (página 6)

to wait: (aguarda) esperar (página 49)

to wake up: despertarse (página 16)

wall: pared (página 14)

to wallpaper: empapelar (página 14)

walnut: nuez (página 44)

to warm up: calentarse (página 86)

to wash: lavar (página 45)

to wash up: fregar (página 19)

washing machine: lavadora (página 18)

water: agua (página 85)

to water: (plantas) regar (página 47)

watering can: regadera (página 47)

watermelon: sandía (página 44)

wave: ola (página 85)

to wave goodbye: despedirse, decir adiós con la mano (página 59)

weak: débil (página 7)

weather: clima, tiempo (página 86)
webbed foot: pata palmeada (página 36)
to weigh: pesar (página 52)
wet: húmedo, -a (página 36)
whale: ballena (página 40)
wheel: rueda, goma (páginas 54, 55 y 59)
wheelbarrow: carretilla (página 47)
to whisk: (claras de huevo, leche) batir (página 19)
whiskers: bigote (página 30)
white: blanco (página 25)
white bean: judía blanca (página 45)
whole: entero, -a (página 11)
wild: salvaje, sin domar (página 31)
wild boar: jabalí (página 41)
to wilt: marchitarse (página 42)
wilted: marchito, -a (página 43)
wind: viento (página 86)
window: ventana (página 14); ventanilla (páginas 57 y 59)
windshield: parabrisas (página 54)
windshield wiper: limpiaparabrisas (página 54)
windy: ventoso, -a (página 86)
wing: ala (páginas 33, 37, 38 y 59)
winter: invierno (página 87)
wintry: invernal (página 87)
wolf: lobo (página 41)
wool: lana (página 32)
wooly: lanudo, -a (página 32)
to work: trabajar (página 52)
worker bee: abeja obrera (página 38)
wrinkled: (de la ropa) arrugado, -a (página 12)
wrist: (parte del brazo) muñeca (página 6)
wristband: muñequera (página 72)
to write: escribir (página 22)

X-ray: radiografía (página 78)
xylophone: xilófono (página 68)

yellow: amarillo (página 25)
young: joven (página 10)
young frog: rana joven (página 36)

zebra: cebra (página 41)
zucchini: calabacín, calabacita (página 45)

a

a la derecha: on the right (pg. 21)
a la izquierda: on the left (pg. 21)
abajo: below (pg. 20)
abeja: bee (pg. 38)
abeto: fir (pg. 42)
abierto, abierta: open (pg. 22)
abogado, abogada: lawyer (pg. 52)
abrazar: to hug (pg. 11)
abrelatas: can opener (pg. 18)
abrocharse: to button up (pg. 12)
abrocharse: to fasten your seatbelt (pg. 59)
abuela: grandmother (pg. 10)
abuelo: grandfather (pg. 10)
aburrido, aburrida: bored (pg. 71)
acampar: to camp (pg. 84)
acantilado: cliff (pg. 85)
acelga: swiss chard (pg. 45)
acera: sidewalk (pg. 49)
acercarse: to approach (pgs. 20 & 83)
acomodador, acomodadora: usher (pg. 66)
acondicionador de aire: air conditioner (pg. 15)
acostarse: to lie down (pg. 6)
actor: actor (pg. 66)
actriz: actress (pg. 66)

adelantarse: to overtake (pg. 20)
adornar: to decorate (pg. 11)
aduana: customs (pgs. 58 & 60)
aeropuerto: airport (pg. 58)
afilados, afiladas: sharp (pg. 35)
agacharse: to crouch (pg. 6)
agalla: gill (pg. 35)
agricultor, agricultora: farmer (pg. 53)
agua: water (pg. 85)
aguijón: stinger (pg. 38)
águila: eagle (pg. 41)
ajo: garlic (pg. 45)
ajo porro: leek (pg. 45)
ala: wing (pgs. 33, 37, 38, & 59)
álamo: poplar (pg. 42)
alarma: alarm (pg. 79)
albañil: bricklayer (pg. 52)
albaricoque: apricot (pg. 44)
alcachofa: artichoke (pg. 45)
alcantarilla: drain (pg. 49)
alejarse: to go away, (pg. 20); to fly away (pg. 83)
aleta: fin (pg. 35), flipper (pg. 73)
alfombra: rug (pg. 15)
alfombra de baño: bath mat (pg. 17)
algodón: cotton balls (pg. 78)
almeja: clam (pg. 40)
almendra: almond (pg. 44)
almohada: pillow (pg. 16)
alto, alta: tall (pgs. 6 & 70)
alumno, alumna: pupil, student (pg. 22)
alunizar: to land (on the moon) (pg. 83)
amable: polite (pg. 49)
amarillo: yellow (pg. 25)
ambulancia: ambulance (pg. 78)
amontonar: to pile up (pg. 87)
amplificador: amplifier (pg. 69)
anaranjado: orange (pg. 24)
ancla: anchor (pg. 61)
andén: platform (pg. 56)
anestesia: anesthetic (pg. 78)
anestesiar: to anesthetize (pg. 78)
anestesista: anesthesiologist (pg. 78)

animado, animada: excited (pg. 71)

animales: animals (pgs. 28, 40, & 41)

antena: antenna (pgs. 37, 38, & 54)

antena de satélite: satellite dish (pg. 14)

antiguo, antigua: vintage (pg. 54)

apagar: to put out, extinguish (pg. 79)

aparatos electrónicos: electrical equipment (pg. 64)

apartamento: apartment (pg. 48)

apio: celery (pg. 45)

aplaudir: to applaud (pg. 66)

aposento: apartment (pg. 48)

apretado, apretada: tight (pg. 13)

arañar: to scratch (pg. 30)

arar: to plough (pg. 84)

árbitro: referee (pgs. 70 & 71)

árboles: trees (pg. 42)

arco iris: rainbow (pgs. 24 & 86)

área de descanso: rest area (pg. 50)

área de servicios: service station (pg. 51)

arena: sand (pg. 85)

armario: closet (pg. 16); cupboard (pg. 19)

aro: hoop (pg. 75)

arpa: harp (pg. 68)

arqueópterix: archaeopteryx (pg. 29)

arriba: above (pg. 20)

arroz: rice (pg. 45)

arrugado, arrugada: wrinkled (pg. 12)

articulaciones: joints (pg.7)

artículos de limpieza: cleaning products (pg. 81)

ascender: to go up (pg. 74)

asiento: seat (pgs. 54, 55, & 57)

asomarse: to lean out (pg. 14)

asteroide: asteroid (pg. 83)

asustadizo, asustadiza: frightened (pg. 30)

atacar: to attack (pg. 35)

aterrizar: to land (pg. 59)

atigrado, atigrada: tawny (pg. 21)

atletismo: athletics (pg. 75)

atracar: to dock (pg. 60)

atrapar: to catch (pg. 39)

aula: classroom (pg. 22)

auriculares: headphones (pg. 64)

autobús: bus (pg. 58)

autopista: highway (pg. 50)

avellana: hazelnut (pg. 44)

avenida: road (pg. 49)

avestruz: ostrich (pg. 41)

avión: airplane (pg. 59)

ayudante de dentista: dental assistant (pg. 77)

azafata: flight attendant (pg. 59)

azucarero: sugar bowl (pg. 19)

azul: blue (pg. 25)

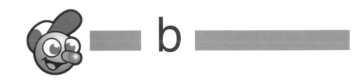

baba: slime (pg. 39)

bailar: to dance (pg. 68)

bajar: to go down (pg. 14)

bajito, bajita: short (pgs. 6 & 70)

balancearse: to swing (pg. 75)

balar: to bleat (pg. 32)

balcón: balcony (pg. 66)

ballena: whale (pg. 40)

baloncesto: basketball (pg. 70)

balsa: air mattress (pg. 85)

banco: bank (pg. 48); bench (pg. 70)

bandeja: tray (pg. 19)

banquillo: bench (pg. 71)

bañarse: to swim (pg. 85)

bañadera: bathtub (pg. 17)

baño: bathroom (pg. 17); restroom (pg. 56)

barbero/peluquero, peluquera: barber/hairdresser (pg. 53)

barbilla: chin (pg. 6)

barco: ship (pg. 61)

barra: bar (pg. 75)

barrer: to sweep (pg. 87)

bastón: pole (pg. 74)

basurero: trash bin (pgs. 14 & 49)

bata: robe (pg. 13)

batería: battery (pg. 54); drum set (pg. 69)

batir: to whisk (pg. 19)

bebidas: drinks (pg. 81)

berenjena: eggplant (pg. 45)

besar: to kiss (pg. 11)

biblioteca: library (pg. 48)

bicicleta: bicycle (pg. 55)

bidé: bidet (pg. 17)

bigote: whiskers (pg. 30)

billete: ticket (pg. 58)

bizcocho de cumpleaños: birthday cake (pg. 11)

blanco: white (pg. 25)

blando, blanda: soft (pg. 9)

bloc: notepad (pg. 23)

blusa: blouse (pg. 12)

boca: mouth (pg. 35)

bocina: speaker (pg.65)

bodega: cargo hold (pg.61)

boina: beret (hat) (pg. 12)

bol: bowl (pg. 18)

boleto: ticket (pg. 56)

bolígrafo: ballpoint pen (pg. 23)

bolsa de compras: grocery bag (pg. 81)

bomba de incendios: fire engine (pg. 79)

bombero: firefighter (pg. 79)

bombón: chocolate (pg. 11)

bonito, bonita: pretty (pg. 43)

borde: edge (pg. 73)

borrador: eraser (pg. 22)

borrar: to erase (pg. 22)

bota: (ski) boot (pg. 74)

botar: to throw away (pg. 48)

bote: boat (pg. 60)

bote salvavidas: lifeboat (pg. 61)

boya: buoy (pg. 60)

braquiosaurio: brachiosaurus (pg. 28)

braza: breaststroke (pg. 73)

brazo: arm (pg. 6)

brillar: to shine (pg. 82)

bronceador: suntan lotion (pg. 85)

broncearse: to sunbathe (pg. 85)

brotar: to sprout (referring to plants) (pg. 87)

bucear: to swim underwater (pg. 73)

butaca: armchair (pg. 15)

buzón: mailbox (pgs. 49 & 80)

C

caballo: horse (pg. 31)

cabeza: head (pgs. 6, 36, 37, & 39)

cabina: cab (pg. 57); cockpit (pg. 59)

cabina de teléfonos: telephone booth (pg. 49)

cacahuate: peanut (pg. 44)

cacarear: to crow (pg. 33)

cactus: cactus (pg. 42)

cadena: chain (pg. 55)

cadera: hip (pg. 6)

café: coffee (pg. 81); brown (pg. 24)

cafetera: coffee maker (pg. 18)

cafetería: café (pg. 48)

caja: cash register (pg. 81)

cajero, cajera: cashier (pg. 81)

calabacín: zucchini (pg. 45)

calamar: squid (pg. 40)

calculadora: calculator (pg. 23)

calentarse: to warm up (pg. 86)

caliente: hot (pg. 9)

calle: street (pg. 49)

calle ruidosa: noisy street (pg. 48)

calle silenciosa: quiet street (pg. 48)

calzoncillo: underpants (pg. 13)

cama: bed (pg. 16)

cámara de televisión: TV camera (pg. 67)

cámara de video: video camera (pg. 65)

cámara fotográfica: camera (pg. 65)

camarón: shrimp (pg. 40)

camarote: cabin (pg. 61)

canicas: marbles (pg. 62)

camello: camel (pg. 31)

camino: path (pg. 46)

camión: truck (pg. 50)

camión de equipaje: baggage truck (pg. 58)

camiseta: T-shirt (pg. 13); shirt (pg. 71)

camisón: nightgown (pg. 13)

campo: playing field (pg. 71); country, field (pg. 84)

canal: slide (pg. 62)

canasta: net (pg. 70)

cancha: court (pg. 72)

cangrejo: crab (pg. 40)

canguro: kangaroo (pg. 41)

canicas: marbles (pg. 62)

canillera: shin guard (pg. 71)

cantar: to sing (pg. 68)

caparazón: shell (pg. 34)

capó: hood (pg. 54)

caracol: snail (pg. 39)

caramelo: candy (pg. 11)

careta submarina: goggles (pg. 73)

carga: cargo (pg. 60)

cargar: to load (pg. 56)

carguero: freighter (pg. 60)

cariñoso, cariñosa: friendly (pg. 30)

carne: meat (pg. 81)

carnicero, carnicera: butcher (pg. 52)

carnívoro, carnívora: carnivorous (pg. 29)

carpeta: three-ring binder (pg. 23)

carretilla: wheelbarrow (pg. 47); dolly (pg. 56)

carril: lane (pg. 50)

carrito de compras: shopping cart (pg. 81)

carro: car (pg. 54)

carro de juguete: toy car (pg. 63)

carta: letter (pg. 80)

cartas: cards (pg. 63)

cartel: poster (pg. 16)

cartero: letter carrier (pg. 80)

casa: house (pg. 14)

casa de muñecas: dollhouse (pg. 63)

casco: hoof (pg. 31); helmet (pgs. 55 & 79)

casete: videocassette (pg. 64)

castañuelas: castanets (pg. 69)

castillo: castle (pg. 63)

catarro: a cold (pg. 76)

catorce: fourteen (pg. 26)

cavar: to dig (pg. 47)

cebolla: onion (pg. 45)

cebra: zebra (pg. 41)

ceja: eyebrow (pg. 9)

cepillarse los dientes: to brush your teeth (pg. 17)

cepillo de dientes: toothbrush (pg. 17)

cerca: near (pg. 20); fence (pgs. 14 & 46)

cereales: cereals (pg. 45)

cereza: cherry (pg. 44)

cerrado, cerrada: closed (pg. 22)

cesta: basket (pg. 81)

champiñón: mushroom (pg. 45)

champú: shampoo (pg. 17)

chaqueta: jacket (pg. 12)

chaqueta impermeable: waterproof jacket (pg. 74)

chimenea: chimney (pg. 14); funnel (pg. 61)

chirimoya: custard apple (pg. 44)

chocar: to crash (pg. 51)

choque: crash, accident (pg. 51)

cien: one hundred (pg. 26)

cinco: five (pg. 26)

cincuenta: fifty (pg. 26)

cine: movie theater (pg. 48)

cinta adhesiva: tape (pg. 78)

cintura: waist (pg. 6)

cinturón: belt (pg. 12)

cinturón de seguridad: seat belt (pg. 54)

círculo: circle (pg. 27)

ciruela: plum (pg. 44)

cirujano, cirujana: surgeon (pg. 78)

ciudad: city (pg. 48)

clarinete: clarinet (pg. 69)

claraboya: porthole (pg. 61)

claro, clara: light (pg. 25)

clavel: carnation (pg. 43)

cliente: customer (pg. 81)

clima: weather (pg. 86)

cobertizo: tool shed (pg. 46)

cobija: blanket (pg. 16)

cocina: kitchen (pg. 18)

cocodrilo: crocodile (pg. 40)

código postal: postal code (pg. 80)

codo: elbow (pg. 6)

coger un tren: to catch a train (pg. 56)

col: cabbage (pg. 45)

cola: tail (pgs. 30, 33, 34, 35, & 59)

colar la pelota: to score (pg. 70)

colchoneta: mat (pg. 75)

colegio: school (pg. 22)

coliflor: cauliflower (pg. 45)

colmena: beehive (pg. 38)

colores: colors (pg. 24)

columna vertebral: spine (pg. 7)

columpiarse: to swing (pg. 62)

columpio: swing (pg. 62)

combustible: fuel (pg. 58)

cometa: comet (pg. 83)

cómodo, cómoda: comfortable (pg. 15)

compás: compass (pg. 23)

comprar: to buy (pg. 48)

compsognathus: compsognathus (pg. 29)

computadora: computer (pg. 16)

concha: shell (pg. 39)

concha enrollada: spiral shell (pg. 39)

conducir: to drive (pg. 54)

conductor: conductor (pg. 57)

congelados: frozen food (pg. 81)

cono: cone (pg. 27)

consigna automática: locker (pg. 56)

constelación: constellation (pg. 82)

construir: to build (pgs. 38 & 63)

consultorio: doctor's office (pg. 76)

contento, contenta: happy (pg. 10)

contrabajo: bass (pg. 68)

control remoto: remote control (pg. 64)

copiloto: copilot (pg. 59)

cordero: lamb (pg. 32)

corral: pen (pgs. 32 & 84)

corredor, corredora: runner (pg. 75)

correr: to run (pgs. 6, 30, & 75)

cortacésped: lawn mower (pg. 47)

cortar: to cut (pgs. 18 & 53)

cortina de baño: shower curtain (pg. 17)

corto, corta: short (pg. 12)

costilla: rib (pg. 7)

cráneo: skull (pg. 7)

crecer: to grow (pg. 42)

cresta: comb (on a hen) (pg. 33)

crin: mane (pg. 31)

crisálida: chrysalis (pg. 37)

crisantemo: chrysanthemum (pg. 43)

croar: to croak (pg. 36)

cruzar: to cross (pg. 49)

cuaderno: notebook (pg. 23)

cuadrado, cuadrada: square (pg. 27)

cuadro: picture (pg. 15)

cuarenta: forty (pg. 26)

cuarto, cuarta: fourth (pg. 26)

cuarto de baño: bathroom (pg. 17)

cuatro: four (pg. 26)

cubierta: deck (pg. 61)

cubilete: (for dice) shaker (pg. 63)

cubo: cube (pg. 27)

cuchara: spoon (pg. 18)

cucharita: teaspoon (pg. 19)

cucharón: ladle (pg. 19)

cuchillo: knife (pg. 18)

cuello: neck (pgs. 6 & 31)

cuerda: jump rope (pg. 62)

cuerno: horn (pg. 32)

cuerpo: body (pg. 6)

cuerpo blando: soft body (pg. 39)

cuidado, cuidada: tidy (pg. 46)

cuidar a un enfermo: to nurse (pg. 76)

curioso, curiosa: curious (pg. 30)

curva: curve (pg. 51)

dados: dice (pg. 63)

dalia: dahlia (pg. 43)

dátil: date (pg. 44)

debajo: under (pg. 20)

débil: weak (pg. 7)

décimo, décima: tenth (pg. 27)

decorado: scenery (pg. 66)

dedo: finger (pg. 6)

dedo del pie: toe (pg. 6)

defensa: bumper (pg. 54)

delante: in front of (pg. 21)

delfín: dolphin (pg. 40)

delgado, delgada: thin (pg. 6)

dentista: dentist (pg. 77)

dentro: in (pg. 21)

deportes: sports (pg. 70)

desabrocharse: to unbutton (pg. 12)

descansar: to rest (pg. 52)

descargar: to unload (pg. 56)

descender: to go down (pg. 74)

descortés: rude (pg. 49)

descuidado, descuidada: untidy (pg. 46)

desembarcar: to disembark (pg. 61)

desenchufar: to unplug (pg. 65)

desinflado, desinflada: deflated (pg. 55)

desordenado, desordenada: messy (pg. 15)

despedirse: to wave goodbye (pg. 59)

despegar: to take off (pg. 59)

despertador: alarm clock (pg. 16)

despertarse: to wake up (pg. 16)

desvestirse: to get undressed (pg. 12)

detenerse: to stop (pg. 55)

detrás: behind (pg. 21)

devolver: to return (pg. 72)

dibujar: to draw (pg. 24)

diccionario: dictionary (pg. 23)

diecinueve: nineteen (pg. 26)

dieciocho: eighteen (pg. 26)

dieciséis: sixteen (pg. 26)

diecisiete: seventeen (pg. 26)

diente: tooth (pgs. 31, 35, & 77)

dientes: teeth (pg. 7)

diez: ten (pg. 26)

diferentes: different (pg. 11)

dinero: money (pg. 81)

dinosaurios: dinosaurs (pg. 28)

diplodoco: diplodocus (pg. 28)

dirección: address (pg. 80)

director, directora: director (pg. 67)

dirigir: to direct (pg. 67)

disco: record (pg. 16)

dividir: to divide (pg. 26)

doblar: to bend (pg. 7); to turn (pg. 50)

doce: twelve (pg. 26)

doctor, doctora: doctor (pg. 76)

dolor de cabeza: headache (pg. 76)

dominó: dominoes (pg. 63)

dormir: to sleep (pg. 16)

dormitorio: bedroom (pg. 16)

dos: two (pg. 26)

driblar: to dribble (pg. 70)

ducha: shower (pg. 17)

ducharse: to take a shower (pg. 17)

durazno: peach (pg. 44)

duro, dura: hard (pg. 9)

echar: to mail (pg. 80)

edredón: comforter (pg. 16)

electricista: electrician (pg. 52)

elefante: elephant (pg. 41)

embarcadero: jetty (pg. 60)

embarcar: to embark (pg. 61)

empapelar: to wallpaper (pg. 14)

empujar: to push (pgs. 15, 54, & 70)

enchufar: to plug in (pg. 65)

encía hinchada: swollen gum (pg. 77)

enciclopedia: encyclopedia (pg. 22)

encima: on (top of), above (pg. 20)

enfermo, enferma: patient (pg. 76)

enfrentarse: to face (pg. 20)

enfrente: in front (pg. 20)

engrapadora: stapler (pg. 23)

engrasar: to oil (pg. 55)

enroscarse: to curl up (pg. 34)

enseñar: to teach (pg. 53); to show (pg. 58)

entero, entera: whole (pg. 11)

entrar: to go in (pg. 66)

entre: between (pg. 21)

entregar: to deliver (pg. 80)

entrenador, entrenadora: coach (pg. 71)

entretenimientos: leisure activities (pg. 62)

equipaje: luggage (pg. 57)

equipo de sonido: stereo system (pg. 16)

escalera: stairs, steps (pg. 14); ladder (pg. 79)

escamas: scales (pgs. 34 & 35)

escapar: to escape (pg. 34)

escarbador: (digging) fork (pg. 47)

escarbar: to scratch (pg. 33)

escenario: stage (pg. 66)

escondite: hide-and-seek (pg. 62)

escribir: to write (pg. 22)

escuchar: to listen (pg. 64)

escurrir: to drain (pg. 45)

esfera: sphere (pg. 27)

espalda: back (pg. 6); backstroke (pg. 73)

espantapájaros: scarecrow (pg. 84)

espantar: to scare (pg. 84)

esparadrapo: tape (pg. 78)

espárrago: asparagus (pg. 45)

espejo: mirror (pg. 17)

espejo retrovisor: (rearview) mirror (pg. 55)

esperar: to wait (pg. 49)

espinaca: spinach (pg. 45)

esponja: sponge (pg. 17)

esqueleto: skeleton (pg. 7)

esquí: skiing (sport) (pg. 74); ski (gear) (pg. 74)

esquiador, esquiadora: skier (pg. 74)

esquiar: to ski (pg. 74)

esquilar: to shear (pg. 32)

esquina: corner (pg. 49)

establo: barn, stable (pg. 84)

estación de bomberos: fire station (pg. 79)

estación de tren: train station (pg. 56)

estación de esquí: ski resort (pg. 74)

estacionar: to park (pg. 50)

estaciones: seasons (pg. 87)

estadio: stadium (pg. 71)

estante: shelf (pg. 81)

estegosaurio: stegosaurus (pg. 29)

esterilla: beach mat (pg. 85)

estetoscopio: stethoscope (pg. 78)

estirarse: to stretch (pg. 7)

estornudar: to sneeze (pg. 76)

estrella: star (pg. 82)

estrella de mar: starfish (pg. 40)

estuche de lápices: pencil case (pg. 23)

estudiar: to study (pg. 22)

estudio de televisión: television studio (pg. 67)

estufa: stove (pg. 19)

examinar: to examine (pg. 76)

explicar: to explain (pg. 58)

exprimidora: juicer (pg. 18)

facturación de equipaje: (baggage) check-in (pg. 58)

falda: skirt (pg. 12)

familia: family (pg. 10)

farmacéutico, farmacéutica: pharmacist (pg. 53)

farmacia: pharmacy (pg. 48)

faro: lighthouse (pg. 60)

farol: streetlight (pg. 49); (car) headlight (pg. 54)

fatigado, fatigada: tired (pg. 70)

fax: fax (pg. 80)

fiambres: cold cuts (pg. 81)

ficha: counter (pg. 63)

fiesta: party (pg. 11)

filmar: to film (pg. 64)

fino, fina: fine (pg. 25)

firmar: to sign (pg. 80)

flamenco: flamingo (pg. 40)
flash: flash (pg. 65)
flauta: flute (pg. 69)
flojo, floja: baggy (pg. 13)
flor: flower (pg. 46)
florecer: to flower (pg. 87)
florero: vase (pg. 18)
flores: flowers (pg.43)
flotar: to float (pgs. 61 & 73)
flotador: rubber ring (pg. 85)
foca: seal (pg. 40)
foco: light (pg. 67)
formas: shapes (pg. 26)
fosa nasal: nostril (pg. 8)
fotocopiadora: photocopier (pg. 22)
fotografiar: to take photos (pgs. 53 & 64)
fotógrafo, fotógrafa: photographer (pg. 53)
frambuesa: raspberry (pg. 44)
fregadero: sink (pg. 18)
fregar: to wash up (pg. 19)
freír: to fry (pg. 19)
frenar: to brake (pg. 54)
freno: brake (pg. 55)
frente: forehead (pg. 6)
fresa: strawberry (pg. 44)
frío, fría: cold (pg. 9)
frutero, frutera: grocer (pg. 52)
frutos: fruits and nuts (pg. 44)
fuente: serving dish (pg. 19)
fuera: out (pg. 21); por fuera: outside (pg. 14)
fuerte: strong (page 7)
fumigar: to spray (pg. 42)
furgón de escalerilla: stair truck (pg. 59)
fútbol: soccer (pg. 71)

gafas: goggles (pg. 74)
galaxia: galaxy (pg. 82)

galletas: cookies (pgs. 11 & 81)
gallina: hen (pg. 33)
galopar: to gallop (pg. 31)
gancho: hanger (pg. 16)
garabatear: to scribble (pg. 24)
garaje: garage (pg. 14)
garra: paw (pg. 30)
gasolinera: gas station (pg. 51)
gato: cat (pg. 30)
gaviota: seagull (pgs. 40 & 85)
gigantesco, gigantesca: gigantic (pg. 29)
gimnasia: gymnastics (pg. 75)
girar: to spin (pg. 7)
giro postal: money order (pg. 80)
globo: balloon (pg. 11)
globo terráqueo: globe (pg. 22)
golpear: to hit (pg. 72)
goma: tire (pg. 55)
goma de borrar: eraser (pg. 23)
gordo, gorda: fat (pg. 6)
gorila: gorilla (pg. 41)
gorra: cap (pgs. 12 & 73)
gorrión: sparrow (pg. 33)
gorro: hat (pg. 11)
gorro de baño: shower cap (pg. 17)
gotero: (eye) dropper (pg. 76)
grabar: to record (pg. 64)
grande: big (pgs. 35 & 55)
granizo: hail (pg. 86)
grifo: faucet (pg. 17)
gris: gray (pgs. 21 & 24)
gritar: to shout (pg. 10)
grúa: tow truck (pg. 51); crane (pg. 60)
grueso, gruesa: thick (pg. 25)
gruñón, gruñona: fierce (pg. 30)
guante: glove (pg. 74)
guiñol: puppet theater (pg. 63)
guirnalda: garland (pg. 11)
guisante: pea (pg. 45)
guitarra eléctrica: electric guitar (pg. 69)

h

haba lima: lima bean (pg. 45)
habichuela: green bean (pg. 45)
hambriento, hambrienta: hungry (pg. 37)
hangar: hangar (pg. 58)
hélice: propeller (pg. 61)
herbívoro, herbívora: herbivorous (pg. 29)
hermana: sister (pg. 10)
hermano: brother (pg. 10)
herramientas: tools (pg. 47)
hervir: to boil (pg. 45)
hiena: hyena (pg. 41)
hierba: grass (pg. 46)
higo: fig (pg. 44)
hijo: son (pg. 10)
hipopótamo: hippopotamus (pg. 40)
hocico: nose (of an animal) (pg. 30)
hoja: leaf (pg. 42)
hombro: shoulder (pg. 6)
horno microonda: microwave oven (pg. 19)
horquilla: (digging) fork (pg. 47)
hortensia: hydrangea (pg. 43)
hospedarse: to stay at (a hotel) (pg. 48)
hospital: hospital (pg. 78)
hotel: hotel (pg. 48)
huesos: bones (pg. 7)
huesudo, huesuda: skinny (pg. 7)
huevo: spawn (pg. 36); egg (pgs. 33 & 37)
hundirse: to sink (pg. 61)

i

iglesia: church (pg. 84)
iguales: same (pg. 11)
incómodo, incómoda: uncomfortable (pg. 15)

inflar: to pump up (pg. 55)
información: information (pg. 56)
injertar: to graft (pg. 42)
inodoro: toilet (pg. 17)
inspeccionar: to inspect (pg. 58)
instrumentos: instruments (pgs. 77 & 78);
instrumentos musicales: musical instruments (pg. 68)
invernadero: greenhouse (pg. 46)
invernal: wintry (pg. 87)
invierno: winter (pg. 87)
iris: iris (pg. 9)

j

jabalí: wild boar (pg. 41)
jabón: soap (pg. 17)
jacinto: hyacinth (pg. 43)
jarabe: syrup (pg. 76)
jardín: garden (pg. 46)
jardín de flores: flower bed (pg. 46)
jardinero: gardener (pg. 46)
jarra: pitcher (pg. 19)
jefe de estación: stationmaster (pg. 56)
jeringuilla: syringe (pg. 78)
jirafa: giraffe (pg. 41)
joroba: hump (pg. 31)
joven: young (pg. 10)
judía blanca: white bean (pg. 45)
juego: game (pg. 62)
juey: crab (pg. 40)
juez: judge (pg. 70)
juez de línea: line judge (pg. 72); linesman (pg. 71)
jugador, jugadora: player (pgs. 70 & 71)
jugar: to play (pg. 63)
jugo: juice (pg. 11)
juguete: toy (pg. 63)
juguetón: playful (pg. 32)
juntos, juntas: close together (pg. 14)

 **k**

kiwi: kiwi (pg. 44)

 **l**

labio: lip (pgs. 9 & 23)
ladrar: to bark (pg. 30)
lamerse: to lick (pg. 30)
lámpara: lamp (pgs. 15, 16, & 77)
lana: wool (pg. 32)
lancha: motorboat (pg. 85)
lanudo, lanuda: woolly (pg. 32)
lanzar: to serve (in tennis) (pg. 72)
lanzarse: to go down (pg. 62)
lápiz: pencil (pg. 23)
largo, larga: long (pg. 12)
larguero: goalpost (pg. 71)
lavabo: sink (pg. 77)
lavadero de carros: car wash (pg. 54)
lavadora: washing machine (pg. 18)
lavamanos: sink (pg. 17)
lavaplatos: dishwasher (pg. 19)
lavar: to wash (pg. 45)
leche: milk (pg. 81)
lechuga: lettuce (pg. 45)
legumbres: legumes (pg. 45)
lejos: far (pg. 20)
lengua: tongue (pgs. 9, 34, & 36)
lenteja: lentil (pg. 45)
lento, lenta: slow (pg. 34)
león: lion (pg. 41)
leopardo: leopard (pg. 41)
leotardos: tights (pg. 12)
levantarse: to get up (pg. 16)
libar: to drink (pg. 38)

libre: freestyle (pg. 73)
librero: bookshelf (pg. 15)
libro: book (pg. 23)
licuadora: blender (pg. 18)
ligero, ligera: light (pgs. 29 & 37)
limón: lemon (pg. 44)
limpiaparabrisas: windshield wiper (pg. 54)
limpio, limpia: clean (pg. 13)
lirio: lily (pg. 43)
llegadas: arrivals (pg. 56)
llanta: tire (pg. 54)
lleno, llena: full (pg. 38)
llorar: to cry (pgs. 10 & 66)
lluvia: rain (pg. 86)
lobo: wolf (pg. 41)
locomotora: engine (pg. 57)
loma: hill (pg. 84)
lomo: back (pgs. 30 & 31)
Luna: moon (pg. 83)

 **m**

madre: mother (pg. 10)
maduro, madura: ripe (pg. 44)
maestro, maestra: teacher (pg. 22)
maíz: sweet corn (pg. 45)
maleta: suitcase (pg. 56)
maletero: (car) trunk (pg. 54); porter (pg. 56)
manantial: spring (pg. 84)
mandarina: tangerine (pg. 44)
mandíbula: jaw (pg. 35)
manejar: to drive (a car) (pg. 54)
manguera: hose (pgs. 47 & 79)
mano: hand (pg. 6)
manso, mansa: tame (pg. 31)
mantel: tablecloth (pg. 19)
manubrio: handlebars (pg. 55)
manzana: apple (pg. 44)
manzano: apple tree (pg. 42)

mapa: map (pg. 22)

maquillar: to put on makeup (pg. 67)

maquinista: engineer (pg. 57)

mar: sea (pg. 85)

maraca: maraca (pg. 69)

marcador: scoreboard (pg. 71)

marchitarse: to wilt (pg. 42)

marchito, marchita: wilted (pg. 43)

marearse: to feel dizzy (pg. 79)

margarita: daisy (pg. 43)

marino, marina: marine (adj.) (pg. 34)

mariposa: butterfly (pg. 37); butterfly stroke (pg. 73)

masajista: trainer (pg. 71)

materiales escolares: school objects (pg. 23)

maullar: to meow (pg. 30)

mecánico: mechanic (pg. 51)

media: sock (pg. 12)

mediano, mediana: medium-sized (pg. 55)

médico, médica: doctor (pg. 76)

mejilla: cheek (pg. 6)

mejillón: mussel (pg. 40)

melón: melon (pg. 44)

mesa: coffee table (pg. 15); table (pg. 18)

mesita de noche: bedside table (pg. 16)

micrófono: microphone (pg. 67)

miel: honey (pg. 38)

mil: one thousand (pg. 26)

millón: one million (pg. 26)

mirar: to look (pg. 49)

mochila: school bag, backpack (pg. 23)

modelo: model (pg. 53)

moderno, moderna: modern (pg. 54)

monitores: monitors (pg. 67)

monopatín: skateboard (pg. 62)

montaña: mountain (pg. 84)

morir: to die (pg. 28)

moteado: spotted; black and white (pg. 21)

moto: motorcycle (pg. 55)

motor: engine (pg. 54); motor (pg. 55)

motor de propulsión: jet engine (pg. 59)

muela cariada: decayed tooth (pg. 77)

muela empastada: filled tooth (pg. 77)

muelle: pier (pg. 60)

mugir: to moo (pg. 32)

multiplicar: to multiply (pg. 26)

muñeca: wrist (pg. 6)

muñeco, muñeca: doll (pg. 63)

muñequera: wristband (pg. 72)

músculos: muscles (pg. 7)

musculoso, musculosa: muscular (pg. 7)

museo: museum (pg. 48)

muslo: thigh (pg. 6)

n

nacer: to hatch (pg. 28)

nadar: to swim (pg. 28)

naranja: orange (pg. 44)

nariz: nose (pg. 8)

natación: swimming (pg. 73)

nave espacial: spaceship (pg. 82)

navegar: to sail (pg. 60)

nebulosa: nebula (pg. 82)

negro: black (pg. 25)

nervioso: nervous (pg. 71)

nevado: snowy (pg. 86)

niebla: fog (pg. 86)

nieve: snow (pg. 86)

nombre: name (pg. 80)

noveno, novena: ninth (pg. 27)

noventa: ninety (pg. 26)

nube: cloud (pg. 86)

nublado, nublada: cloudy (pg. 86)

nueve: nine (pg. 26)

nuevo, nueva: new (pg. 14)

nuez: walnut (pg. 44)

números: numbers (pg. 26)

 o

 p

obediente: obedient (pg. 32)

obrera: worker bee (pg. 38)

ochenta: eighty (pg. 26)

ocho: eight (pg. 26)

octavo, octava: eighth (pg. 27)

ocultarse: to hide (pg. 39); to set (the sun) (pg. 82)

oficina de correos: post office (pg. 80)

oír: to hear (pg. 8)

ojo: eye (pgs. 9, 30, 35, 37, & 39)

ojos saltones: bulging eyes (pg. 36)

ola: wave (pg. 85)

oler: to smell (pg. 8)

olivo: olive tree (pg. 42)

olmo: elm (pg. 42)

once: eleven (pg. 26)

operar: to operate (pg. 78)

ordenado, ordenada: tidy (pg. 15)

ordenar: to tidy up (pg. 63)

ordeñar: to milk (pg. 32)

oreja: ear (pgs. 8 & 30)

órgano eléctrico: electric keyboard (pgs. 65 & 68)

orquesta: orchestra (pg. 66)

oruga: caterpillar (pg. 37)

oscuro, oscura: dark (pg. 25)

oso: bear (pg. 41)

oso de peluche: teddy bear (pg. 63)

otoñal: autumnal (pg. 87)

otoño: autumn (pg. 87)

oveja: sheep (pg. 32)

paciente: patient (pg. 78)

padre: father (pg. 10)

paja: straw (pg. 33)

pala: shovel (pg. 47)

palco: box (pg. 66)

paleta: trowel (pg. 47)

palmera: palm (pg. 42)

pan: bread (pg. 81)

panal: honeycomb (pg. 38)

pandereta: tambourine (pg. 69)

panel de información: information board (pg. 56)

panera: bread basket (pg. 19)

pantalla: screen (pg. 66)

pantalón: pants (pgs. 12 & 74)

pantaloncito: panties (pg. 13)

pantalón (de esquí): ski pants (pg. 74)

pantorrilla: calf (pg. 6)

pantufla: slipper (pg. 13)

papa: potato (pg. 45)

papagayo: parrot (pg. 41)

papalote: kite (pg. 62)

papel higiénico: toilet paper (pg. 17)

paquete: package (pg. 80)

parabrisas: windshield (pg. 54)

paralelas: parallel bars (pg. 75)

parar: to stop (pg. 51); to save (pg. 71)

parasaurolophus: parasaurolophus (pg. 28)

pardo: brown (pg. 21)

pared: wall (pg. 14)

párpado: eyelid (pgs. 9 & 34)

partido, partida: cut (pg. 11)

pasajero, pasajera: passenger (pgs. 57 & 59)

pasaporte: passport (pg. 58)

pasar: to pass (pgs. 50 & 70); to go through (pg. 75)

pasillo: aisle (pgs. 59 & 66)

paso de peatones: crosswalk (pg. 49)

pasta de dientes: toothpaste (pg. 17)

pastelitos: pastries (pg. 11)

pastor: shepherd (pg. 84)

pata: leg (pgs. 34 & 36)

pata delantera: front leg (pg. 30)

pata palmeada: webbed foot (pg. 36)

pata trasera: hind leg (pg. 30)

patear: to kick (pg. 71)

patines de ruedas: roller skates (pg. 62)

patinar: to skate (pg. 62)

peaje: toll booth (pg. 51)

pecho: chest (pg. 6)

pedal: pedal (pg. 55)

pedalear: to pedal (pg. 55)

pedir: to ask for (pg. 48)

pegajoso, pegajosa: sticky (pg. 36)

peinarse: to comb your hair (pg. 17)

peine: comb (pg. 17)

pelar: to peel (pg. 19)

película: film (pg. 66)

peligroso, peligrosa: dangerous (pg. 49)

pelo: fur (pg. 30)

pelota: ball (pgs. 70, 71 & 72)

pensamiento: pansy (pg. 43)

pepino: cucumber (pg. 45)

pequeño, pequeña: small (pgs. 35 & 55)

pera: pear (pg. 44)

perder un tren: to miss a train (pg. 56)

perejil: parsley (pg. 45)

perfumado, perfumada: sweet smelling (pg. 43)

periodista: reporter (pg. 53)

perrera: doghouse (pg. 14)

perro: dog (pg. 30)

perseguir: to chase (pg. 34)

persiana: blind (pg. 16)

pesado, pesada: heavy (pg. 29)

pesar: to weigh (pg. 52)

pescadero, pescadera: fish dealer (pg. 52)

pescado: fish (pg. 81)

pescador: fisher (pg. 53)

pescar: to fish (pgs. 35 & 53)

pesquero: fishing boat (pg. 60)

pestañas: eyelashes (pg. 9)

pétalo: petal (pg. 43)

petrolero: oil tanker (pg. 60)

petunia: petunia (pg. 43)

pez espada: swordfish (pg. 40)

pezuña: hoof (pg. 32)

piano: piano (pg. 68)

piar: to tweet (pg. 33)

picar: to chop (pg. 18); to sting (pg. 38)

pico: beak (pg. 33)

picotear: to peck (pg. 33)

pie: foot (pg. 6)

piel: skin (pgs. 8 & 36); hide (pg. 32)

piel húmeda: wet skin (pg. 36)

pierna: leg (pg. 6)

pijama: pajamas (pg. 13)

pila: battery (pg. 65)

píldoras: pills (pg. 76)

piloto: pilot (pg. 59)

pimiento rojo: red pepper (pg. 45)

pingüino: penguin (pg. 40)

pino: pine (pg. 42)

pintar: to paint (pg. 24)

pintor: painter (pg. 53)

piña: pineapple (pg. 44)

piñón: pine nut (pg. 44)

piscina: pool (pg. 73)

pista de aterrizar: runway (pg. 58)

pista de esquí: downhill ski trail (pg. 74)

pista para carreras: running track (pg. 75)

pista de coches: car racetrack (pg. 63)

pistacho: pistachio (pg. 44)

pitar: to blow the whistle (pg. 71)

pizarrón: blackboard (pg. 22)

planchado, planchada: ironed (pg. 12)

planeta: planet (pg. 83)

plantas: plants (pg. 42)

plantar: to plant (pg. 47)

plastilina: modeling clay (pg. 23)

plátano: banana (pg. 44)

platillo: cymbal (pg. 69)

plato llano: plate (pg. 18)

plato hondo: soup bowl (pg. 18)

playa: beach (pg. 85)

plomero: plumber (pg. 52)

pluma: feather (pg. 33)

pluma fuente: fountain pen (pg. 23)

pocilga: pigsty (pg. 84)

podrido, podrida: rotten (pg. 44)

policía: police officer (pg. 50)

pollito: chick (pg. 33)

pomada: ointment (pg. 76)

poncharse: to puncture (pg. 54)

ponerse: to put on (pg. 13)

popa: stern (pg. 61)

portaequipaje: luggage rack (pg. 57)

portería: goal (pg. 71)

portero: goalkeeper (pg. 71)

potro: foal (pg. 31); horse (in gymnastics) (pg. 75)

presentador, presentadora: announcer (pg. 67)

presentar: to announce (pg. 67)

presilla: paper clip (pg. 23)

primavera: spring (pg. 87)

primaveral: springlike (pg. 87)

primero, primera: first (pg. 26)

primo, prima: cousin (pg. 10)

proa: prow (pg. 61)

probar: to taste (pg. 8)

profesor, profesora: teacher (pg. 52)

proyector: projector (pg. 22)

público: audience (pg. 66); spectators (pg. 71)

pueblo: village (pg. 84)

puente: bridge (pg. 50)

puente de peatones: footbridge (pg. 50)

puerta: door (pg. 14)

puerto: port (pg. 60)

pulpo: octopus (pg. 39)

pupila: pupil (pg. 9)

pupitre: desk (pg. 22)

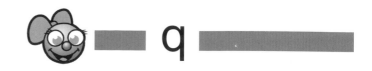

querer: to love (pg. 10)

quesos: cheese (pg. 81)

quince: fifteen (pg. 26)

quinto, quinta: fifth (pg. 26)

quiosco: newsstand (pg. 49)

quirófano: operating room (pg. 78)

quitarse: to take off (pg. 13)

rábano: radish (pg. 45)

radar: radar (pgs. 58 & 61)

radiador: radiator (pg. 15)

radio: radio (pg. 65)

radiocasete personal: personal radio cassette player (pg. 64)

radiocasetera: radio cassette player (pg. 16)

radiografía: X-ray (pg. 78)

raíz: root (pg. 42)

rallador: grater (pg. 18)

rallar: to grate (pg. 18)

rama: branch (pg. 42)

rana: frog (pg. 36)

rana joven: young frog (pg. 36)

rápido: fast (pg. 54)

raqueta: racquet (pg. 72)

rascacielos: skyscraper (pg. 48)

rasguear: to strum (pg. 69)

rastrillo: rake (pg. 47)

rayo: lightning (pg. 86)

rebanar: to slice (pg 45)

rebaño: flock (pgs. 32 & 84)

receta: prescription (pg. 76)

recortado, recortada: trimmed (pg. 46)

recortar: to cut out (pg. 22)
recostarse: to lie down (pg. 15)
rectangular: rectangular (pg. 27)
rectángulo: rectangle (pg. 27)
red: net (pgs. 71 & 72)
redondo, redonda: round (pg. 27)
refrescarse: to cool down (pg. 86)
refrigerador: refrigerator (pg. 18)
regadera: watering can (pg. 47)
regalar: to give a gift (pg. 11)
regalo: gift (pg. 11)
regar: to water (pg. 47)
regla: ruler (pg. 23)
reina: queen bee (pg. 38)
reír: to laugh (pgs. 10 & 66)
relámpago: lightning (pg. 86)
relinchar: to neigh (pg. 31)
reloj: clock (pgs. 22 & 56)
remar: to row (pg. 85)
remolacha: beet (pg. 45)
remolcador: tugboat (pg. 60)
remolcar: to tow (pg. 51)
renacuajo: tadpole (pg. 36)
reptar: to slither (pg. 34)
resbaladilla: slide (pg. 62)
resbaladizo, resbaladiza: slippery (pg. 35)
resbalarse: to slip (pg. 86)
rescatar: to rescue (pg. 79)
respirar: to breathe (pg. 73)
restar: to subtract (pg. 26)
revolver: to stir (pg. 18)
río: river (pg. 84)
roble: oak (pg. 42)
robot: robot (pg. 63)
rodilla: knee (pg. 6)
rodillera: knee pad (pg. 70)
rojo: red (pg. 25)
rompecabezas: puzzle (pg. 63)
rompeolas: breakwater (pg. 85)
ropa: clothes (pg. 12)
rosa: rose (flower) (pg. 43)
rosado: pink (pg. 24)
rubio, rubia: fair (referring to physical appearance) (pg. 6)

rueda: wheel (pg. 54)
ruedas: wheels (pg. 59)
ruidoso, ruidosa: noisy (pgs. 10 & 48)

S

sábana: sheet (pg. 16)
sacacorchos: corkscrew (pg. 18)
sacapuntas: pencil sharpener (pg. 23)
sacudir: to shake (pg. 69)
sala: living room (pg. 15)
sala de máquinas: engine room (pg. 61)
sala de emergencias: emergency room (pg. 78)
salidas: departures (pg. 56)
salir: to come out (pg. 66)
salir (el sol): to rise (the sun) (pg. 82)
saltar: to jump (pgs. 6, 36, 74, & 75)
salto de altura: high jump (pg. 75)
salto con garrocha: pole vault (pg. 75)
salud: health (pg. 76)
salvaje: wild (pg. 31)
salvavidas: lifeguard (pg. 85)
sandía: watermelon (pg. 44)
sardina: sardine (pg. 35)
satélite artificial: satellite (pg. 83)
saxofón: saxophone (pg. 69)
secador (de pelo): hairdryer (pg. 17)
secarse: to dry yourself (pg. 17); to wilt (pg. 42)
segundo, segunda: second (pg. 26)
seguro: lock (car) (pg. 54)
seguro, segura: safe (pg. 49)
seis: six (pg. 26)
seleccionar: to change (channels) (pg. 65)
sellar: to stamp (pg. 80)
sello: stamp (pg. 80)
semáforo: traffic light (pg. 49)
sembrar: to sow (pg. 84)
semilla: seed (pg. 46)

sentidos: senses (pg. 8)

sentido del gusto: sense of taste (pg. 9)

sentido del oído: sense of hearing (pg. 8)

sentido del olfato: sense of smell (pg. 8)

sentido de la vista: sense of sight (pg. 9)

sentido del tacto: sense of touch (pg. 8)

señal de tráfico: road sign (pg. 50)

separado, separada: far apart (pg. 14)

séptimo, séptima: seventh (pg. 27)

serpiente: snake (pg. 34)

servicios: services (pg. 78)

servilleta: napkin (pg. 19)

sesenta: sixty (pg. 26)

setenta: seventy (pg. 26)

seto: hedge (pg. 46)

sexto, sexta: sixth (pg. 27)

siete: seven (pg. 26)

silla: chair (pgs. 15 & 77)

silla de playa: beach lounger (pg. 85)

silo: silo (pg. 84)

sirena: siren (pg. 78)

sobre: envelope (pg. 80)

sobrecama: bedspread (pg. 16)

sofá: sofa (pg. 15)

Sol: sun (pg. 82)

soleado: sunny (pg. 86)

sombrilla de playa: beach umbrella (pg. 85)

sopera: tureen (pg. 19)

soplar: to blow (pg. 69)

subibaja: seesaw (pg. 62)

subir: to go up (pg. 14)

sucio, sucia: dirty (pg. 13)

sudar: to sweat (pg. 86)

suéter: sweater (pg. 12)

sumar: to add (pg. 26)

sumergirse: to dive underwater (pg. 39)

supermercado: supermarket (pg. 81)

suplente: substitute (pg. 70)

 t

tabla de surf: surfboard (pg. 85)

tablero: board game (pg. 63); backboard (pg. 70)

tablón de anuncios: bulletin board (pg. 22)

taladro: drill (pg. 77)

tallo: stalk (pg. 43)

tambor: drum (pg. 69)

taquilla: ticket office (pg. 56)

tarjeta de crédito: credit card (pg. 81)

tarjeta postal: postcard (pg. 80)

taxista: taxi driver (pg. 53)

taza: cup (pg. 19)

té: tea (pg. 81)

teatro: theater (pgs. 48 & 66)

techo: roof (pg. 14); ceiling (pg. 16)

técnico de sonido: sound engineer (pg. 67)

tejado: roof (pg. 14)

teléfono: telephone (pg. 15)

telesilla: chair lift (pg. 74)

televisor: television (set) (pgs. 15 & 64)

telón: curtain (pg. 66)

tenderse: to lie down (pg. 6)

tendones: tendons (pg. 7)

tenedor: fork (pg. 18)

tenis: tennis (pg. 72)

tenista: (tennis) player (pg. 72)

tentáculo: tentacle (pg. 39)

tercero, tercera: third (pg. 26)

termómetro: thermometer (pg. 76)

ternero: calf (pg. 32)

terrestre: land (adj.) (pg. 34)

tetera: teapot (pg. 19)

tía: aunt (pg. 10)

tiburón: shark (pg. 35)

tiempo: weather (pg. 86)

tienda: shop (pg. 49)

tierra: soil (pg. 46)

Tierra: earth (pg. 83)

tigre: tiger (pg. 41)

tijeras podadoras: clippers (pg. 47)
timbal: kettle drum (pg. 68)
timbre: doorbell (pg. 14); bell (pg. 55)
timón: steering wheel (pg. 54); rudder (pg. 61)
tío: uncle (pg. 10)
tiranosaurio: tyrannosaurus (pg. 29)
tirar: to throw (pg. 71)
tirar a la basura: to throw away (pg. 48)
tiza: chalk (pg. 22)
toalla: towel (pgs. 17 & 85)
tobillo: ankle (pg. 6)
tobogán: slide (pg. 62)
tocadiscos: record player (pg. 22)
tocar: to touch (pg. 8); to ring (a bell) (pg. 15); to play (an instrument) (pg. 65)
tomar el pulso: to take a pulse (pg. 78)
tomate: tomato (pg. 45)
tormenta: thunderstorm (pg. 86)
toronja: grapefruit (pg. 44)
torre de control: control tower (pg. 58)
tortuga: tortoise (pg. 34)
toser: to cough (pg. 76)
tostadora: toaster (pg. 19)
trabajador, trabajadora: hardworking (pg. 38)
trabajar: to work (pg. 52)
trabajo: job (pgs. 52 & 53)
tractor: tractor (pg. 84)
tragar: to swallow (pg. 35)
traje de baño: swimsuit (pg. 73)
trampolín: diving board (pg. 73)
tranquilo, tranquila: quiet, calm (pg. 10)
transformarse: to turn into (pg. 36)
transporte: transportation (pg. 54)
trece: thirteen (pg. 26)
treinta: thirty (pg. 26)
tren: train (pgs. 56 & 57)
tren de carga: freight train (pg. 57)
tren de pasajeros: passenger train (pg. 57)
tren subterráneo: subway (pg. 48)
trepar: to climb (pg. 62)
tres: three (pg. 26)
triangular: triangular (pg. 27)
triángulo: triangle (pg. 27)
triceratops: triceratops (pg. 28)

triciclo: tricycle (pg. 62)
trigueño, trigueña: dark (pg. 6)
triste: sad (pg. 10)
trombón: trombone (pg. 69)
trompeta: trumpet (pg. 69)
tronco: trunk (of the body) (pg. 36); (tree) trunk (pg. 42)
trotar: to trot (pg. 31)
trusa: swimming trunks (pg. 73)
tubo de escape: exhaust pipe (pg. 55)
tulipán: tulip (pg. 43)
túnel: tunnel (pg. 50)

ubre: udder (pg. 32)
universo: universe (pg. 82)
uno: one (pg. 26)
untarse bronceador: to put on suntan lotion (pg. 85)
uña: claw (pgs. 33 & 34)
utensilios: (kitchen) utensils (pg. 19)
uva: grape (pg. 44)

vaca: cow (pg. 32)
vacío, vacía: empty (pg. 38)
vagón de literas: sleeping car (pg. 57)
vagón restaurante: dining car (pg. 57)
vaso: glass (pg. 18)
vaso desechable: disposable cup (pg. 77)
vegetal: vegetable (pg. 45)
veinte: twenty (pg. 26)
vela: candle (pg. 11)

velero: sailboat (pg. 60)

vendar: to bandage (pg. 52)

venenoso, venenosa: poisonous (pg. 34)

ventana: window (pg. 14)

ventanilla: window (pgs. 57, 59 & 80)

ventosa: sucker (pg. 39)

ventoso: windy (pg. 86)

ver: to see (pg. 8)

veraniego: summery (pg. 87)

verano: summer (pg. 87)

verde: green (color) (pg. 24); unripe (fruit) (pg. 44)

verdura: vegetable (pg. 81)

vestirse: to get dressed (pg. 12)

veterinario, veterinaria: veterinarian (pg. 52)

vía: (train) track (pg. 57)

videocasete: videocassette (pg. 64)

videocasetera: VCR (pg. 64)

videoconsola: video game (pg. 64)

videojuego: video game (pg. 63)

viejo, vieja: old (pgs. 10 & 14)

viento: wind (pg. 86)

vigilar: to look out (pg. 35)

violeta: purple (pg. 25); violet (flower) (pg. 43)

violín: violin (pg. 68)

violonchelo: cello (pg. 68)

vistoso, vistosa: colorful (pg. 37)

volar: to fly (pgs. 28 & 59)

vomitar: to throw up (pg. 76)

zambullirse: to dive (pgs. 36 & 73)

zanahoria: carrot (pg. 45)

zángano: drone (pg. 38)

zapatear: to tap your feet (pg. 68)

zapato: shoe (pg. 12)

zapato deportivo: athletic shoe (pgs. 12, 70, & 71)

zarpar: to set sail (pg. 60)

zona de peatones: pedestrian zone (pg. 48)

xilófono: xylophone (pg. 68)

128